Better Homes and Gardens®

YOUR FLOORS & STAIRS

BETTER HOMES AND GARDENS® BOOKS

Editor: Gerald M. Knox
Art Director: Ernest Shelton
Managing Editor: David A. Kirchner

Associate Art Directors: Linda Ford Vermie,
Neoma Alt West, Randall Yontz
Copy and Production Editors: Marsha Jahns,
Mary Helen Schiltz, Carl Voss, David A. Walsh
Assistant Art Directors: Harijs Priekulis, Tom Wegner
Senior Graphic Designers: Alisann Dixon, Lynda Haupert,
Lyne Neymeyer
Graphic Designers: Mike Burns, Mike Eagleton, Deb Miner,
Stan Sams, D. Greg Thompson, Darla Whipple

Vice President, Editorial Director: Doris Eby
Group Editorial Services Director: Duane L. Gregg

General Manager: Fred Stines
Director of Publishing: Robert B. Nelson
Vice President, Retail Marketing: Jamie Martin
Vice President, Direct Marketing: Arthur Heydendael

All About Your House: Your Floors and Stairs
Project Editor: James A. Hufnagel
Associate Editor: Willa Rosenblatt Speiser
Assistant Editor: Leonore A. Levy
Copy and Production Editor: David A. Walsh
Building and Remodeling Editor: Joan McCloskey
Furnishings and Design Editor: Shirley Van Zante
Money Management and Features Editor: Margaret Daly

Associate Art Director: Neoma Alt West
Graphic Designer: Stan Sams

Contributing Editors: Jill Abeloe Mead, Stephen Mead
Contributing Senior Writer: Paul Kitzke
Contributors: Karol Brookhouser, Mary Bryson,
Denise L. Caringer, Cathy Howard, Leonore A. Levy,
Willa Speiser, Peter A. Stephano

Special thanks to Ron Hawbaker, William Hopkins,
Bill Hopkins, Jr., Babs Klein, and Don Wipperman for
their valuable contributions to this book.

INTRODUCTION

Have you ever tried to imagine a house without floors? You can't, of course, because the mechanics of gravity demand that we have something to walk on. Floors—and their upwardly mobile cousins, stairs—provide that and much more.

Consider, for example, how floors and stairways set a home's overall tone. Whether you choose to cover them edge to edge with plush carpet or prefer to show off bare wood, how you treat your floors makes a big difference in the way spaces look and live. Upkeep and safety count, too, especially when you realize that you probably devote back-bending energy to cleaning and maintaining what's underfoot, and that a slip, especially on a stairway, can lead to a nasty fall.

Your Floors & Stairs looks at the floors and stairs in your home from many different perspectives. Here you'll learn how to make floors and stairs look their best, how to select surfacing materials from a kaleidoscope of choices, and how to plan floor and stair changes that can totally transform your house. You'll also find information about installing new materials and even an entire staircase, accomplishing repair and refinishing projects, improving the safety and convenience of floors and stairs, and making it easier for a disabled person to move around in your home.

With more than 100 color photographs, plus dozens of drawings, plans, and charts, *Your Floors & Stairs* takes you, step by step, across each of your home's floors and up and down its stairways. If you enjoy the tour, you may want to look into other volumes in the **ALL ABOUT YOUR HOUSE** Library. This comprehensive series of books, from the editors of Better Homes and Gardens®, presents ideas, information, and inspiration to help you make the most of every element and area of your home.

YOUR FLOORS & STAIRS

CONTENTS

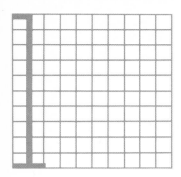

EVALUATING YOUR FLOORS AND STAIRS

Probably the only times you actively notice the floors in your home are when they squeak, need cleaning, are unexpectedly slippery, or look especially nice thanks to a shaft of sunlight or a recent buffing. Not so when you enter someone else's home—floors play a big part in anyone's first impression. Much the same is true of stairs, with an added concern for safety—stairs can be dangerous. In this chapter, we'll start you thinking about the decorative and functional aspects of the floors and stairs in your home; in later chapters, you'll find suggestions for getting the most out of the floors and stairs you now have, and planning and carrying out changes.

COULD NEW FLOORING CHANGE THE LOOK OF YOUR HOUSE?

You've just repainted the cabinets in your 1940s kitchen, repapered the walls, and made new curtains, but the kitchen still seems dated. If you find yourself in a similar predicament, take a look at the floor. Sometimes being clean just isn't enough. For example, vintage linoleum that's 40 years old may be in decent condition, but it probably will never look fresh and appealing again. Replacing flooring could brighten the whole room, set an entirely new decorative mood, and lighten floor-cleaning chores.

Just replacing time-worn flooring with something new can work a remodeling miracle. And when this is combined with other surface changes, such as painting, papering, and new hardware, the result often looks much greater than the sum of its parts.

New flooring need not be different flooring. Sometimes the flooring you have is just right, but simply looks tired; replacing it with a similar or even identical material could make a big difference. But if you're going to the trouble and expense of installing new flooring, why not explore all the possibilities and come up with an entirely new look? Perhaps a hard surface, such as quarry tile, would do wonders for your kitchen, and be less costly and complicated to install than you might think.

For more about the look and effects you can achieve with the myriad materials available today, see Chapter 2—"Flooring Ideas: Making a Statement." If you have a general idea about the kind of flooring you want but are unsure how to judge quality, see chapters 5 and 6—"Choosing and Buying Soft Floor Coverings" and "Choosing and Buying Other Flooring Materials."

There's more than one way to floor a floor

The honey-colored hardwood floor in the living room pictured *opposite* is not the home's original flooring. It sets a gracious, traditional mood, however, in a way that threadbare carpeting could not. The warm, red Oriental rug that's the room's centerpiece is a valuable decorative element here, too. It brings color to a restfully neutral scheme, and provides an anchor for the room's main seating group.

Of course, wood topped with a rug isn't the only way to go, even in formal areas such as this living room. Consider how the room would look if it were carpeted from wall to wall in rich, deep-tone plush. Or think about how a different hard-surface material, such as terra-cotta paving tile, could create a dramatic change in the room's decorative mood.

Looks are one matter, function is another. If yours is a home with active toddlers or pets, area rugs that easily skitter out from underfoot might constantly need straightening, and also present a safety hazard. Cleanability is an important factor, too, especially in heavily trafficked zones. Since you can probably achieve the look you want with any of several different materials, choose the one most appropriate for a room's function and for your life-style. More about this on the pages that follow.

IS YOUR STAIRCASE A FOCAL POINT?

If you live in a single-level house, the only stairs you have may be purely functional—perhaps a sturdy but dull flight leading to the basement, or a now-you-see-it, now-you-don't disappearing staircase that leads to attic crawl space. If, on the other hand, you live in a multilevel house, the stairs are likely to be a major presence. Not only do you spend a lot of time going up and down them, but they are in full view, often taking center stage in a center hall.

If your staircases—or staircase—are not behind closed doors, they almost automatically become focal points of the room they're in. They are large, they dramatically link the parallel planes of floor and ceiling, and they lead the eye upward: In short, they're very much *there*.

With this inherent star quality to work with, there's no reason why the main staircase in your home should not be a decorative highlight. Warmly polished wood, appealing color contrasts and combinations, colorful runners, even a mini art gallery—all can add interest and charm to a staircase. The examples pictured here show just two ways to turn a necessary up-and-down passageway into a thing of beauty.

The traditionally styled switchback staircase shown *at right* provides a fine visual focal point in a room that's already full of appealing things to look at. Bright yellow walls all along the stairway add zest to the more subdued tones of the brick wall and floor. The blue-and-yellow quilt—an original from the 1800s—accents the color scheme from its position on the wall above the second flight of stairs.

Incidentally, as long-established as these stairs look, they and the rest of the house are new. The home's exterior is in the New England saltbox style, but the interior, as the stairway design and decor suggest, is open and contemporary in plan.

For more about the various types of staircases, and the styles and visual effects you can achieve with each, see Chapter 3—"Stairways: Connecting Two Levels." If you'd like to concentrate your decorating efforts on the stairs themselves, rather than the overall staircase, turn to pages 42 and 43 for information about stair runners.

The dramatic open-riser stairway pictured *opposite* is something of a hybrid. The banister and newel post are recycled mahogany pieces, rescued from another building. The other stairway elements are new. And the result of the combination is striking.

The house itself was built in the 1940s, and the stairway is a replacement for the original. In the course of a whole-house renovation, these stairs were carefully planned to provide visual interest in their own right, yet not interfere with the view from the dining room into the home's back garden. Besides the dramatic open silhouette of the stairs, room exists below the staircase for an eye-catching display of plants and a whimsical horse-and-buggy weather vane.

If you plan to replace existing stairs or build new stairs in the course of a major remodeling or adding-on project, you'll find ideas and advice in Chapter 4—"Planning Floor and Stair Changes."

EVALUATING YOUR FLOORS AND STAIRS

COULD NEW FLOORING LESSEN HOUSEWORK?

Scrub. Sweep. Vacuum. Wax. Replace a broken tile. Resand a patch under a once-leaking ceiling. Floors, like all other elements of your home, require maintenance to look their best. And because floors get such heavy use, it sometimes seems that taking care of them occupies a disproportionate amount of housekeeping time. Short of barring traffic in all but one or two rooms, or covering walkways with plastic, nothing will make your floors completely maintenance free. You may, however, be able to minimize housekeeping chores by selecting low-maintenance flooring and by applying long-term protective finishes to materials that might otherwise call for frequent attention.

Some floors look dirty as soon as they're walked on; others camouflage dirt and look good for days between cleanings. Several factors make the difference: material, finish, and color are key elements.

Some materials, of course, are designed to thrive with only minimal attention. Resilients are probably the best known of these. Many types of carpeting, too, lend themselves to a low-maintenance approach, although very light and very dark colors both show dirt more readily than intermediate shades do.

There are ways to make other materials easier to care for, too. For example, if you have oil-finished wood floors in your home and feel that you spend more time than you'd like caring for them, consider switching to a polyurethane coating. This will involve sanding and refinishing, but once that's done the floor will have greater resistance to spills and wear. The parquet floor in the entrance hallway pictured *at left* is an example of how to handle a material that's not traditionally easy to care for. Because it's coated with several layers of polyurethane, it's hardly more likely to be damaged by frequent traffic or wet feet than a ceramic floor would be. For information about choosing finishes and refinishing wood floors, see pages 120-121 and 138-139.

To learn more about selecting flooring that's right for the areas you have in mind, turn to pages 66-73 in Chapter 4. For more about the maintenance requirements of various flooring materials, see chapters 5 and 6. Pages 150 and 151 give cleaning tips.

HOW SAFE ARE YOUR FLOORS AND STAIRS?

Because stairs and floors are so familiar, we don't always realize that they can be hazardous. Tripping on stairs or slipping on a loose scatter rug may not seem as dramatically dangerous as falling out of an apple tree or slipping on a patch of ice in a sleet storm, but the painful result is the same. A few precautions and a little common sense go a long way toward making sure that your floors and stairs are as hazard-free as possible.

The stairway shown *at left* is very handsome. It is also very solid and safe. The carpeted treads have a low pile that provides traction without loose threads that might catch at heels; the newel posts and balusters are sturdy, so that anyone who does happen to slip will have something substantial to catch on to. And the railing behind the dining table ensures that no one will carelessly step into the well of the lower stairway.

Whatever the material and style of your stairway, keeping it free of obstacles, well-lit, adequately railed, and as skid-proof as possible is the key to safety. Even a fairly minor change in level can be disconcerting and increase the chances of tripping or falling. For that reason, two or three stairs leading from one room to another, or from the interior to the exterior, call for many of the same extra safety features as a full-length staircase.

Floors, although they offer large expanses of level surface, offer a few special problems of their own. Beware of slippery conditions caused by a too-slick finish, spilled liquids, or an unstable rug. Unexpected obstacles and broken surfaces in need of repair are other culprits.

Chapter 10—"Safety and Service"—tells you how to make sure your floors and stairs will work their best for you and your family. To learn more about repairing potentially hazardous conditions, see Chapter 9—"Repairing and Refinishing Floors and Stairs."

WHERE'S THE BEST LOCATION FOR A NEW STAIRWAY?

In some cases, the new stairway you're planning may simply be a replacement for an existing stairway that's either so unattractive or so unsound that it can't be fixed. If traffic patterns and room layouts are satisfactory and no other major remodeling is planned, the best place for this kind of new stairway is probably just where the old one was. If, however, you are building a new stairway because of major changes in your home's floor plan, or because you are building a new house, the question is much more complex. It would be nice to say that you can put a new stairway anywhere you want, but it's not quite that simple. On this page we'll give you a few reasons why.

No matter what their style and no matter how innovative your new layout, stairs must be convenient, accessible, and safe. Because most stairways are by nature heavy traffic areas, any new stairway should be as centrally located as possible—the lasting popularity of the center-hall Colonial scheme, for example, has as much to do with its convenience as with its appealing styling.

When you are planning to relocate a staircase or are thinking about the best location for a new one, keep several points in mind.

• Any space with a staircase in it, whether a hallway or a regular room, is going to lose a certain amount of usable area to traffic. Can you afford to give up this kind of space in a living room or family room? Could moving a stairway out of such a room and into a hallway open up much-needed living space?

• Would moving your staircase improve life on the upper floor of your home? For example, if sounds drift up an open stairway, or traffic upstairs disturbs sleepers in one or more bedrooms, would relocating the stairway solve these problems?

• Can your new stairway do something besides carry up-and-down traffic? For example, could you gain storage space underneath the stairs? The open-riser portion of the stairway pictured at right is an example of usable space tucked under the stairs—in this instance, an auxiliary table near the wet bar. Another possibility, and one with a long history, is a conventional closed storage closet under the stairs.

• Could a new stairway add to your home's architectural interest? For example, if you are

building a contemporary-style home, a handsome wood spiral staircase in the living room might be a dramatic focal point.

• Would you like your new stairway to get natural light during the day? An added aesthetic advantage of a window on a stairway wall or landing is the shaft of light that will light up the room or hallway below. You'll still need artificial light for nighttime and dark days, of course, but a windowed stairway can be a pleasant touch.

• You will have to plan your stairs so they meet the regulations established by local codes; these include the maximum number of steps in a flight, the maximum angle for a staircase, and minimum step sizes. Building code considerations also influence certain aspects of stair location. For example, if you have or plan to have very high ceilings, you will probably need more steps than the code allows in a single straight run. In that case, you'll have to plan a switchback staircase or one with a landing in the middle. Your house may have only one or two places that can accommodate a stairway of those dimensions.

If you're planning to remodel your home and expect to replace an existing stairway, see pages 74 and 75 for more information. For more about stairs and their traffic patterns in general, whether in a remodeled setting or a completely new one, see pages 76-81. To learn more about building new stairs, see Chapter 8—"Installing New Staircases."

CAN YOU CHANGE LEVELS WHEN YOU ADD ON?

If you're planning an addition, you may be wondering how to gain the most floor space with the least possible change in the exterior appearance of your home. You may be fortunate enough to have an attic that can easily be expanded by means of dormers, or a large, level backyard that would welcome a master bedroom wing with hardly a bucket of earth to be moved. If, however, you are planning to add a second or third story where none now exists, or contemplating an addition on a hilly lot, you'll need to incorporate at least a short flight of stairs into your plans. Although changing levels may add to the complexity and perhaps the expense of your adding-on project, it could also make it more interesting. Don't let a hill or too-close lot line stand in your way.

When the owners of the spacious sun-room pictured *at left* decided that the main living areas of their home were too cramped and dark, they looked outward for the solution. The end of the wood-strip flooring in the foreground of the picture marks the place where an exterior wall of the house once stood. On the other side of that wall was a standard wood deck, reached from another part of the house.

The deck, however, was several feet lower than the home's main level. Converting the deck space to a full-fledged room—without scrapping the deck's existing framing—meant accommodating the change in level.

The owners made a virtue out of this necessity by installing an attractive L-shaped set of stairs to link the main living area to the new sun-room. These steps are good looking—and safe, because the wood floors of the original part of the house and white ceramic tile flooring in the new room make it easy to detect the change in levels.

Small changes

To build an addition on a hilly lot or take over existing patio or deck space for a new room, you probably won't need more than a few steps to negotiate the change in levels. Where you choose to put the steps in such a case would most likely hinge on where the old exterior wall or walls are.

In a situation like this, the main question is often largely aesthetic: What do you want the transitional area to look like? Do you want to emphasize the difference in level, or would you prefer to achieve a smooth transition from one to another? Flooring materials and floor coverings will tell the story. For more about choosing floor coverings for a new room, stair hall, or entryway, see chapters 5 and 6; if you plan to install the new flooring yourself or supervise its installation, see Chapter 7—"Installing New Flooring Materials"—for pointers.

Leaps and bounds

If you are converting a rarely used attic to a full-fledged upper story, or adding a completely new upper story, you're going to have to plan and install a whole new stairway. As we noted on the page 14, you need to keep in mind that full stairways take up space, both at top and at bottom.

Consider where on the lower level you can most comfortably give up floor and air space. To take up as little room as possible, you may want to consider installing a spiral staircase. Also think about where on the new upper level you'd prefer traffic to center. Will you need an upstairs hall to direct traffic away from new sleeping areas, for example? For more about planning flooring and stair changes in an addition, see pages 78-81.

In most cases, other than simple basement or attic stairs, building a new staircase is a demanding job that requires the skills of a professional or a highly skilled do-it-yourselfer. If you plan to install a prefabricated spiral staircase, however, you may very well be able to tackle that task on your own; see pages 128-131 for more about that.

COULD SPECIAL FLOOR TREATMENTS HELP YOU DEFINE SPACES?

Sunken living rooms, marble halls, luxuriously piled carpets, jewellike Oriental rugs: Special floor designs such as these can augment an open-plan home by telling you—without walls—where one area ends and another begins. And even if your home doesn't have an open plan, special floor treatments can give rooms a look and feel of luxury. Whatever the reason, if you'd like to do something out of the ordinary with the floors in your home, here are a few points to ponder.

The skylit, plant-accented living room pictured *at right* would be an appealing space even if its floor were flush with the surrounding rooms. Thanks to its two-step-deep recess, however, it is a dramatically defined center of attention.

As you can see, different flooring treatments also help separate the living room from both the dining room in the foreground and the family room on the other side of the floating divider behind the living room. The use of warm-tone quarry tile on the steps leading down to the living room gives that space something of the quality of an indoor patio. The hardwood floor in the living and dining rooms, topped with soft-textured area rugs, further defines the spaces and adds the look—and feel—of luxury underfoot.

If you'd like to have a room or two in your home at a slightly different level than the rest of the structure, you may be able to achieve this effect by building simple but sturdy platforms along the sides of the room. Another possibility: Raise the entire floor in one room a foot or two, giving you a raised rather than a sunken room; this is feasible only where ceilings are unusually high. See page 30 for an example of a raised room.

If you are planning an addition, you may achieve a sunken or recessed effect by necessity as much as by choice. For example, if your extension is a bit downhill from the main part of the house, the project is ideal for a sunken living or family room effect, as discussed on the preceding page.

Special floors

Often you can make a floor look special with nothing more than a change in floor covering. For example, one good handcrafted rug, such as a braided oval or an Oriental rectangle, strategically placed in a living room conversation area will set a decorative mood that extends far beyond the dimensions of the rug itself. Similarly, a full-floor carpet in an unusual color or with an especially soft texture is a luxurious but not necessarily costly or difficult way to make an out-of-the-ordinary decorative statement. See page 41 for an example of how well-placed rugs can turn a floor treatment into a work of art.

In other cases, materials that might be too costly or difficult to maintain over a large expanse of floor are ideal for smaller areas such as entries, hallways, or baths.

Marble, for example, can make almost any hallway elegant, although it does require more careful maintenance than ceramic tile would. Flagstone, quarry tile, and even brick—all natural materials with appealing textures and distinctive colors—can look great in a kitchen, and give other high-traffic, high-visibility rooms special charm.

Although some natural materials are initially more costly than manufactured materials such as vinyl flooring, and may be more difficult to install, you may find the added visual interest and durability well worth the extra effort. For more about using flooring to set a special decorative theme, see pages 44 and 45.

WHICH KITCHEN FLOORING IS BEST FOR YOU?

You and the rest of your family very likely spend a great deal of time in the kitchen—working, eating, and just being together. Your kitchen floor works hard while all this is going on. It regularly experiences traffic and spills and bumps. Does it also look good, and add to the good looks of the rest of your kitchen, or does it remain in the background, subdued if not dreary? If you're planning to update or refresh your kitchen in the near future, you probably already are thinking about new flooring materials. Even if you plan no major redo, however, you may discover that a new kitchen floor could work wonders in a hard-working room.

The crisp chessboard-pattern vinyl-tile flooring pictured *at left* adds sparkle to its spacious, white-and-neutral-dominated surroundings. It's also easy to maintain, comfortable to stand on for long periods of time, and highly durable. In short, this kitchen floor does a variety of jobs very well.

Although resilient flooring—usually but not always made of vinyl—remains a popular choice for kitchen flooring, the possibilities don't end there. Wood, ceramics, stone, and even rubber are among the practical and appealing alternatives. The choice you make depends on the look you want, how much you can spend, and how much care you expect to give the flooring.

For example, you may yearn for the warm look of wood but wonder if wood will hold up under spatters and spills. Or you may want the colorful charm and appealing texture of ceramic tile to brighten your kitchen floor but feel that tile is a luxury material, costly to purchase and difficult to install. In both cases, you can achieve the look you want with the materials you prefer—provided you do your home-work. For information about evaluating and planning for new kitchen flooring materials, see pages 70 and 71.

Successful kitchen flooring must do more than just look good when new. Heavy traffic and frequent drips or spills make for lots of wear and tear on the floor, as well as slip-pery conditions and tripping hazards. For tips on keeping floors clean, safe, and in good condition, see pages 148-151.

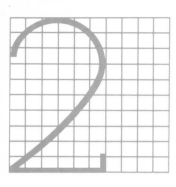

FLOORING IDEAS: MAKING A STATEMENT

Because they provide a highly visible setting for furnishings and accessories, your floors and the coverings you choose for them anchor the rest of your decor. Pine planks, for example, set a decidedly country mood; geometric-patterned area rugs, on the other hand, add a note of casual sophistication. In this chapter, we'll show you a wide variety of flooring ideas, from wall-to-wall carpet to ceramic tiles to hallway runners—floor coverings for every room in your house.

CARPET OPTIONS

Of all the flooring options available today, carpet leads the way in popularity. And no wonder: Not only does carpet offer easy maintenance underfoot, it also provides beauty, softness, and sound absorption.

Another nice thing about carpet is its versatility. You can choose thick and plush carpet for formal elegance, or select a smoother, flatter, level-loop type to enhance a simple, contemporary setting. The contemporary living room pictured *at right,* for example, gains much of its warm, comfortable ambience from wall-to-wall carpet. The covering's soft but subtle texture and warm, neutral color provide an appealing counterpoint to the rustic ceiling beams and smooth, white walls.

Carpet is, by definition, installed over a cushion and tacked or otherwise attached to the floor. It's usually installed wall to wall, although it need not be. It doesn't have to stop where the floor does, either. You can run carpet up the walls for tactile appeal and to reduce noise, or even use it to cover platform furniture.

Carpet offers so much variety, in fact, that deciding what to buy can be intimidating. It's easier to narrow your choices if you first decide what you want your carpet to accomplish. Do you want to add color to your room? Or do you have fine artwork and furnishings that you'd like to showcase against a plain backdrop? Do you have a dull, nondescript space that could benefit from a little texture or pattern? Once you've answered these questions, the next step is to choose the carpet style that's right for you.

(continued)

FLOORING
IDEAS:
MAKING
A STATEMENT

CARPET
OPTIONS
(continued)

Wall-to-wall carpet is ideal for small rooms or homes, where its uninterrupted flow creates a smooth sweep of space underfoot. Solids in light to medium shades do this especially effectively. Use the same color of wall-to-wall carpet in adjacent rooms (say, from your living room and down a hallway leading to the bedrooms), and you'll increase the space-expanding effect.

If making your rooms feel larger isn't a top priority, you have more latitude in selecting carpet colors and patterns. For oversize rooms, or even small ones where coziness rather than spaciousness is desirable, a dark color—a rich jewel-tone green or burgundy, for instance—or a patterned carpet will add warmth and beauty.

Color can alter the feel of your rooms in other ways, too. A warm color will give a sunny feeling to a room with less-than-abundant natural light; a cool blue or green carpet, on the other hand, will tone down an overly sunny space.

As important as your carpet's color is its texture. The living room pictured *opposite* is a good case in point. Since the owners wanted to showcase the styling of their contemporary furnishings, a plain-textured, neutral-toned carpet was the obvious choice. But what kind of carpet? The answer was this level-loop commercial style; its heathery texture as well as its dark yet unobtrusive color contributes warmth and richness to what could have been a cold, austere scheme.

Similarly, sisal carpet squares provide a rough, woven flooring that's perfect for the casual family room shown *above*. The squares' alternating checkerboard pattern and subtle zigzag texture play up their fibrous quality and add tactile interest to an otherwise plain and untextured decorating scheme.

"Carpet" that isn't
If you want the look of carpet without its permanence, think in terms of room-size rugs.

These are really loose-laid carpets, and are available either cut to size from rolls up to 15 feet wide or as budget-pleasing sale-price remnants of wall-to-wall carpeting. Room-size rugs give you the smooth, one-piece look of wall-to-wall carpet, but you can roll them up and take them with you when you move. They're economical, too, because you can turn them to distribute wear.

If your room is a perfect square or rectangle, have the carpet cut to the exact floor size; if the dimensions you're dealing with are less regular, you will probably have to approximate. Keep in mind, however, that room-size rugs usually look best when cut to within a foot of the room's perimeter.

To learn more about choosing carpet, see pages 84-87; for information about laying carpet, turn to pages 108 and 109.

FLOORING IDEAS: MAKING A STATEMENT

WOOD

Nothing warms a room visually like the golden tones and rich grain of a wood floor. Wood isn't just beautiful, either. It's durable, readily available, pleasant to touch as well as to see, and a good insulating material. Best of all, the variety of wood floors available today means you're sure to find one that will work beautifully with any decorating style, and most budgets.

Although wood flooring may cost a bit more than some other flooring options, it will pay you back with lifelong service as well as beauty. Today's polyurethane finishes and woods impregnated with plastic also ensure easy upkeep.

Several types of wood floorings predominate; here's a brief rundown of those most frequently used.

• *Strip flooring* is the most common. Generally oak, these tongue-and-groove wood strips create a floor made up of matching boards, usually about 2½ inches wide. Strip floors are striking in their simplicity, as the glowing example *at left* illustrates. Both prefinished and unfinished wood strips are available.

• *Plank flooring* is wider—up to 12 inches—and offers country-style charm. Planks are usually nailed into place next to each other, and are not necessarily tongue-and-grooved. Pine is the most common material, and it can be very durable.

• *Block flooring* consists of thin blocks of wood made up of either solid wood or plywood laminated with a particular wood. Some block flooring is designed to look like parquet.

• *Parquet flooring* is made of small pieces of wood arranged in geometric patterns. Do-it-yourself parquet tiles, usually 12-inch squares, can be installed for about the cost of standard wall-to-wall carpet. Both do-it-yourself and professionally installed parquet offer perhaps the most interesting design possibilities of any type of wood flooring. Some parquet squares provide a practical advantage, too: They have foam backing for extra insulation. *(continued)*

WOOD
(continued)

I f oak, pine, teakwood, or other conventional wood flooring types are out of your price range, and you think your skills aren't up to installing parquet tiles, don't give up on the idea of wood floors. Waferwood, a durable chipboard with large flakes of wood in it, is available at lumberyards and home centers at a fraction of the cost of other wood flooring. Wafer-wood can be cut into 2-foot squares, then glued and nailed over your present subfloor.

Finishing touches

Whatever type of wood flooring you choose, the finish you select for it can dramatically alter its appearance. For a light-toned country casual effect like that in the bedroom pictured *above,* opt for a sealer and several coats of poly-urethane over oak or pine. Use a medium or dark stain on the same floor, and you'll achieve a traditional, decades-old richness of surface. In the elegant dining room pictured *opposite,* the parquet floor is especially striking, thanks to the rich color of the wood strips in each square.

Bleaching is another floor-coloring option, but one best left to professionals because of the caustic chemicals required.

Another option, especially for badly worn older floors or for new softwood floors, is paint. Use long-wearing deck paint, or ordinary enamel topped with polyurethane.

When it comes to painted floors, a solid color is the most common and often the safest choice. But you also can have fun in an attic, playroom, or child's room by painting boards in a rainbow of colors.

Another possibility is to re-create a bit of early Americana with a spatter-painted floor. To do this, use a stiff-bristled whisk broom to make spatters of one color over a floor you've painted another color.

One of today's most distinctive wood-floor finishes consists of stenciling designs over an existing finish. Buy precut stencils at a specialty shop, or create your own design and cut it out of stiff paper. To paint stenciling, simply dip your brush in the paint and dab—don't stroke—the paint through the stencil. For two examples of stenciling, see the photos on pages 44 and 45.

For more about selecting and installing wood flooring, turn to pages 100-103 and 116-121.

HARD-SURFACE FLOORING

Whether you prefer the handcrafted flavor of Southwestern-style decorating or the cool elegance of contemporary styling, you can find a hard-surface flooring material to suit your taste. Available in designs that range from mellow Mexican squares and rustic country bricks to straightforward geometric shapes with glossy, glazed finishes, hard-surface materials make a durable and striking decorative statement.

As the contemporary, gallerylike hallway and living room pictured *at left* show, traditional hard-surface floorings such as bricks or brick-shaped quarry tiles work as well in a modern setting as in a country-style room. Here the large, architecturally interesting space could have seemed *too* large, cold, and forbidding if warm-toned, rough-textured half-bricks had not been called into play. Whether you choose half-bricks, quarry tile, adobe tile, or colorfully glazed squares, a hard-surface floor can go a long way toward establishing the mood you want in your rooms.

Here's a brief rundown of the basic types of hard-surface flooring.
• *Clay tile* comes in two forms, ceramic and quarry tile. Ceramic tiles are available in many glazes, patterns, colors, and shapes. Quarry tiles are fired from clay in natural tones such as terra-cotta.
• *Marble,* in squares of various sizes, and *slate,* in precut squares and rectangles, offer a choice of gray, blue, red, green, or black, among other possibilities.
• Less-common hard-surface flooring materials include *Mexican adobe tiles* and *concrete tiles;* the latter can be stained and sealed to resemble the more expensive adobe.

Most hard-surface floors, except marble, are impervious to water, grease, and other stains. Some tiles are subject to cracking and chipping if a hard, heavy object falls on them, but it's fairly easy to remove a broken tile and replace it with a new one. Many ceramic tiles and bricks also can be used outdoors.
(continued)

HARD-SURFACE FLOORING
(continued)

Because of their small size and modular method of arrangement, tiles of all types lend themselves to a wide variety of designs. Even bricks of the same color can be set in a wide range of eye-pleasing patterns. Ceramic materials, which come in more varied colors and shapes than bricks do, offer even greater aesthetic possibilities.

Quarry tile, for example, comes in many sizes, shapes, and colors. Some tiles, like the hexagonal ones that dress up the dining area pictured *opposite,* offer an inherently beautiful pattern even without color variations. To take full

advantage of tiles with this kind of visual appeal, it's best to keep other surfaces simple and other patterns in the room to a minimum. For example, the unadorned white walls and cathedral ceiling of the dining area make its tile floor all the more dramatic.

To emphasize the shape and layout of the tiles, use grout of a contrasting color. Here, the warm brown color and geometric shape of the tiles show up especially well against white grout. Conversely, you can buy grout tinted to match hard-surface materials, a good choice if you want a uniform look.

Geometric progressions
Plain square tiles, like those in the carefully designed kitchen shown *above,* also have a lot to offer. Here, the glazed squares create a dramatic grid—and an easy-care surface as well. Used this way, the tiles are elegant enough to flow from the kitchen right into an adjacent dining room or living area.

Simple squares like these also can create special, patterned effects when used in combination with other tile shapes or colors. For instance, lay black and white squares on the diagonal for a diamond pattern, then add a solid

border of half-tiles; surround large tile squares with smaller squares; or create wide bands of stripes across or around a room.

Geometric flooring is a creative way to minimize a room's flaws. A narrow room, for example, will seem wider if you break it up with a pattern of stripes or diagonals across it, and a shoebox-style room with few architectural details will gain interest and charm with a creative floor design.

For more about hard-surface floorings, see pages 96-99 and 104-107.

FLOORING IDEAS: MAKING A STATEMENT

RESILIENT FLOORING

Resilient flooring is usually easier on the budget than carpet, wood, and hard-surface flooring. Additionally, resilients can stand up to almost any punishment, from falling objects to tracked-in dirt and mud. Best of all, they offer handsome styling and can be installed over almost any type of subfloor.

Resilient flooring is generally made of vinyl, either solid or blended with other materials. As its name implies, it has a bit of "give" in it for extra comfort and damage resistance. Resilience adds to the durability of resilient flooring, helping it retain its good looks for years.

Choosing resilient flooring doesn't mean giving up the creative possibilities that ceramic flooring offers; in fact, resilients are available in tile as well as sheet form. In addition, many sheet vinyls offer the look of natural materials, such as brick or stone, at a fraction of the cost of the real thing.

Sheet flooring is among the most popular types of resilient flooring. Because sheet vinyl comes in rolls as wide as 12 feet, you can use it to create a seamless expanse of color and pattern in many rooms.

The most durable of the sheet goods is *inlaid vinyl*. Although more costly than some other vinyl floor coverings, inlaid vinyl offers longer wear and deeper color and texture because the color and pattern go all the way through to the backing.

In *rotovinyl* coverings, photographic images of materials such as slate, wood, or stone are printed on the vinyl, which then is coated with clear vinyl or polyurethane. Rotovinyl floors can be good looking but usually do not last as long as inlaid vinyls.

The tile-look kitchen floor pictured *at right* is an example of resilient sheet flooring at its best. What looks like tile is a seamless sheet of grid-patterned vinyl. The grid adds just the right touch of texture to the floor, sets off the wood tones of the cabinets, and furthers the room's slick, contemporary styling.

(continued)

RESILIENT FLOORING
(continued)

Resilient tile flooring, like sheet flooring, can be solid vinyl or vinyl blended with other materials. You can also buy resilient tiles made of rubber. Here's a brief look at the types available.

• *Solid vinyl tiles* and *rubber tiles* are the two most expensive and the most durable. With vinyl you can choose handsome solids and geometric patterns as well as realistic-looking brick, slate, and quarry-tile designs.

• *Rubber tiles*, popular for a while just after World War II, have made a comeback. The new versions feature raised circle and diamond patterns in a limited range of colors. Wearability is excellent, and today's new rubber tiles further a high-tech, utilitarian look.

• *Vinyl asbestos tiles* are very durable, and moderately priced. With solid-color vinyl asbestos tiles, you can let your imagination have free rein and come up with elegant checkerboard patterns, as well as colorful graphic designs.

• New *vinyl-composition tiles* offer even greater durability than vinyl asbestos tiles do.

Color, pattern, or both?
Keeping color and pattern in mind is as important when you select resilient tile flooring as it is in choosing sheet flooring.

As with any other floor covering, vinyl tiles in light tones and pattern-free designs will help to open up a space; dark, brightly colored, or busily patterned designs will make a room feel smaller and cozier.

The rubber tiles used to smooth the visual passage from kitchen to dining area in the view shown *opposite* are effective for several reasons. Their rich color works well with both the light walls and the natural-wood cabinets. Their subtle texture adds interest without overpowering the passageway. And because the same flooring material is used in two distinct activity centers, the spaces seem to flow into each other, creating a seemingly open floor plan without actually bringing the kitchen into the dining room.

Resilient tiles can add to a distinctive decorative mood, too. The bright, dramatic Mexican-style pattern in the family room shown *above* works with the terra-cotta-colored wall to create a warm, cozy atmosphere.

For more about choosing resilient flooring, see pages 92-95; to learn about installing it, turn to pages 110-113.

FLOORING IDEAS: MAKING A STATEMENT

AREA RUGS

Area rugs are perhaps the most versatile and eye-appealing of all floor coverings. Used atop wood, hard-surface or resilient flooring, or even wall-to-wall carpet, an area rug adds color and pattern to a room in one bold stroke. Whether your taste runs to jewel-toned Oriental rectangles or country-style braided ovals, area rugs warm up rooms with color, pattern, and texture.

Take a look at the attractive conversation grouping shown *at right*. Now imagine how bland the space would be without the added zest the dhurrie rug provides.

The classic way to use an area rug is to place it at the center of a well-polished wood floor. As you can see here, however, a rug can top off virtually any other floor covering. Just make sure patterns don't clash or overpower the room.

An area rug can be more than just an attention getter. It's also the easiest floor covering to use when you want to visually separate one part of your house from another. For example, in the open-plan living room pictured here, the flat-weave rug sets the conversation area apart from an adjacent dining area (not shown).

Another advantage of area rugs is their mobility. For example, you can purchase a 6x9-foot rug knowing that when you move you can simply roll it up and take it along. And because many area rugs are moderate in size, they're flexible; most will easily fit into at least one room in your next home.

If you are interested in purchasing the best quality possible but are concerned about your budget, area rugs give you an excellent way to invest in top-of-the-line floor coverings. Rather than paying for installation of an expensive wall-to-wall carpet, you can choose a small, high-quality area rug to highlight your decorating scheme.

(continued)

AREA RUGS
(continued)

If you have a particularly attractive wood or tile floor but still want some comfort and warmth underfoot, area rugs can contribute just the right touch of softness and pattern without covering up all the flooring. For example in the room pictured *above,* a room-size rug with a patterned border adds plushness without totally hiding the handsome parquet floor.

Area rugs go well not just with other floor materials and coverings, but also with each other. In the dazzling living room pictured *opposite* no fewer than four different rugs play off beautifully against the dramatic architecture—and one of them serves as a bridge to the adjacent room, which features yet another rug. The trick with using multiple area rugs is to vary their sizes, patterns, and colors. Here a very large Portuguese needlepoint rug anchors one seating group, a smaller Oriental rug next to it defines another, and a small square mat serves as a stepping-stone to the patio.

Almost limitless variety
Whether you want an area rug to complement your existing decorating scheme or to set the tone for an entirely new color palette, you'll find an exciting array of colors, patterns, materials, and prices to choose from. Available for the budget-minded are natural-fiber rugs, as well as woven cotton dhurries and machine-made rag and braided rugs in fresh new colors.

If Oriental rugs appeal to you, you can choose between hand-knotted originals and less-costly machine-made versions. Kilims—flat weaves with bright colors and geometric designs—and wool dhurries—in lovely pastels with geometric or animal designs on them—also are popular and widely available.

For more about choosing and buying area rugs, see pages 88-91.

STAIR AND HALL RUNNERS

You can open up a space-deficient foyer, widen a skinny hallway, or brighten an attention-starved stairway with a good-looking runner. Runners are long, narrow area rugs whose change in proportion helps turn small or awkward spaces into striking decorative assets.

As the three attractive passageways pictured here prove, runners offer an instant and affordable way to perk up spaces that might otherwise be forgotten or overlooked.

Add punch to bland spaces
The new-home entryway pictured *above* was bland and colorless when the home was built. Although the space desperately needed eye-appealing accessories, the homeowners found that little floor and wall space was available for furniture or decorative highlights.

The solution? A contemporary, geometrically patterned rug now gives decorative punch and instant character to the previously neutral area.

The rug adds color, pattern, texture, and more. Anchored by double-stick carpet tape, the rug also contributes sure-footed safety to a potentially hazardous, slippery-when-wet entryway.

Direct the eye with a runner
Even a carpeted stairway can benefit from a brightly colored runner. The stairway pictured *opposite, left,* gains a great deal of visual interest from its Oriental-style runner. Here, the neutral-tone carpet visually widens the stairway, and the

vivid runner draws the eye up and into the open living room.

When you use a runner like this, be sure it's color-keyed to the adjacent area, if that area is visible from the stairs and vice versa. In this case, the living room (partially visible) includes several bright-red accents that complement the runner.

A custom-fitted runner is a good solution on odd-size stairways. It's particularly useful for staircases that are too long to be covered by a standard, ready-made runner.

On the gracious old-house stairway pictured *above, right,* the carpet runner, which is cushioned with thick padding underneath, adds safety and comfort underfoot. Because the runner is narrow, it allows a partial view of the mellow old wood treads. The runner also adds a welcome touch of rich color to the setting.

Let a runner fool the eye

Runners can be great deceivers. For example, in a setting where two chairs face each other across a coffee table, you can use a runner beneath the chairs and table to tie them together and create a conversation grouping. Or emphasize the dramatic effect of a diagonal arrangement by placing a 10- or 12-foot runner beneath some of the angled furniture pieces.

A strategically placed runner can help a narrow room seem wider, just as it can a hallway or stairway. Try positioning one across rather than through a tunnel-shape room; you'll be surprised at how the room's proportions seem to change.

ALTERNATIVE DESIGN AND PATTERN IDEAS

Resilients, wood, tile, carpets, area rugs, and runners are just the beginning when it comes to appealing floor coverings. With a little creativity, you can combine those common elements into uncommon and highly personalized treatments for your floors. Here are a few out-of-the-ordinary ideas to spark your imagination.

Early American colonists stenciled their floors and their walls because rugs and wallpaper were expensive and hard to find. Today, home-owners use stencils because of their homespun appeal, as well as the unlimited design possibilities that stenciling affords.

A combination of bleaching, stenciling, and freehand painting created the dining room "rug" shown *opposite.* The design was sealed with several coats of polyurethane, which was followed by a coat of paste wax.

This paint treatment features a border, as does the wall-to-wall carpet pictured *below.*

Here a tricolor border of blue, khaki, and gold sets off an otherwise plain white carpet. The effect is dramatic and elegant but does not over-power the room's other decorative accessories.

A border can do more than add color. It also can help to emphasize a room's interesting shape, as the tricolor border does. Or, perhaps your room doesn't have much built-in distinction and needs inter-esting angles to give it a special personality. If the room is very large, use a border to visually break up the expanse of floor.

Although you can work with an interior designer to have your carpet custom-woven with the border you choose, there is a money-saving alternative to this course of action. Be your own designer: Once you've settled on a design and color, have a skilled carpet-layer piece to-gether two or more carpets to create the border you want.

Another way to create the effect of a custom-made border is to inlay different materials, such as resilient tiles in the center and wood around the edges, or—as mentioned on page 33—a combination of hard-surface floorings. Consider, also, combining wood parquet with strips or planks.

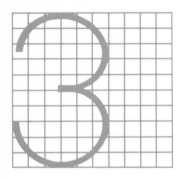

STAIRWAYS: CONNECTING TWO LEVELS

Stairs are among the most functional features of any home. You can't get from one level to the next without them. For all their practical importance, however, they are also key decorative elements. Most stairways are not tucked away behind attic or basement doors, but are right out in the open, in your entrance hall or living room. Styles and types range from simple straight-run stairs to space-saving spirals and switchbacks. Whether you're planning to build new stairs or replace shaky ones, or are looking for ways to spruce up existing stairs, knowing the aesthetic and functional highlights of the various possibilities will help you choose the best type for your home and life-style.

THE GRAND ENTRANCE

The classic grand entrance is a stage set for Scarlett O'Hara: a high-ceilinged center hall with glittering chandeliers and a graceful sweep from ceiling to floor. Few things are more impressive than a wide-open space that welcomes guests to a dramatic view of the best your home has to offer.

To be grand, an entrance needn't be a *Gone with the Wind* remake, however. The key ingredient is a view from top to bottom, an interplay of space on the different levels the stairway connects. Once that's taken care of, the shape and style—even the size of the stairway and its immediate surroundings—are up to you.

The switchback stairs pictured *opposite,* for example, provide an appealing glimpse of upstairs space, punctuated by a midlevel landing. The warm wood tones of the treads and railing contrast strikingly with the flawless white walls and balusters. The entrance hall and its stairway now are a carefully orchestrated room composition, made all the more interesting thanks to the furniture group that's tucked against the lower stairwall.

Old and new

As successful as this entrance is in creating a gracious and expansive mood, it is only one of many possible approaches. A house of the same vintage could have a monochromatic color scheme for a smooth transition to the upper levels of the house, or it could be treated with bright and dramatic colors for a refreshing change-of-pace welcome.

Sometimes the stairs are so intrinsically grand in scope and design that they make a powerful statement without additional decorating. If you are fortunate enough to have a large entrance hall, sweeping antebellum stairs, or a striking contemporary hall and stair combination rich in intriguing angles, you already have a grand entrance. See page 49 for an example of a spectacular new-look entrance.

Other entrances call for accessories before they acquire the importance they should have. Interesting lighting fixtures add drama; wall hangings, plants, rugs, and other decorative extras take on special importance when they share the spotlight with a stairway in your main entrance. Put together a composition using each element of your entry to turn the whole into a grand design. For a glowing example, see page 48.

Look both ways

Your first interest may be in creating an entrance that's impressive and appealing from below—but consider, too, the view from the stairs. Guests as well as family members will experience the view from above nearly as often as they do the one from below, and the perspective will differ greatly.

To enhance the entrance when viewed from above, appeal to the eye level of someone who's on the stairs. The oval-framed print in the photograph *opposite,* for example, provides emphasis and interest as much for a person on the stairs as for one just entering the hallway.

(continued)

THE GRAND ENTRANCE

(continued)

The intensely Victorian entrance hall shown *at right* is in the grand tradition. It's paneled with richly polished, handsomely carved wood and embellished with majestic wall stenciling. This example clearly qualifies as a grand entrance, even though it lacks the width and sweep and swirl of the prototype.

Elaborate detailing rather than size gives this stair hall its elegant effect. Rich colors and textures make a strong initial impression. A complexly patterned rug adds to that. Even seemingly minor accessories such as the light fixtures and flower-topped pedestal contribute to the feeling that this is a place of substance and importance.

Note that with all the attention clearly given to this entrance's appearance, safety and convenience were not sacrificed. Perhaps most significant, the railings and newel posts of these sturdy antique stairways are as strong as they are beautiful. Because the stairs are steep and narrow, solid railings are vital in case of falls, and these perform perfectly.

Floor safety is another key feature. Here, the hallway runner is nowhere near the bottom of the upper staircase or the top of the lower one. This means there's every opportunity to enjoy the runner's visual effect and no chance of a dangerous fall at a stairway's end.

The lighting, too, serves a dual function. The hanging fixture near the door lights the entire space, and the small wall sconce provides accent light and illuminates the potentially treacherous area at the head of the lower stairs.

The brick-and-natural-wood entry pictured *above* is a dramatic example of a grand entrance that owes everything to the present and future. Large clerestory windows cast light from unexpected angles, and provide views of the outside from all levels of the entry. For a person standing at the top of the stairs, these windows offer a vista of treetops; the view down through the

open-plan railing provides a bird's-eye look at the interior of the home.

The entrance offers comparable variety from below. When you walk in the door, a pair of staircases introduces the house. One, not shown, leads down. The stairs shown here lead to the living room/bedroom level of the house, so family members and guests often use them.

In this entry, as in the one on the opposite page, safety and practicality are as important as good looks. During the day, the abundant windows provide ample light; an overhead fixture, not shown here, provides nonglaring illumination after nightfall.

Note that uncarpeted wood treads like these can present a slipping hazard. If you'd like

a bare-wood look, don't coat stairs with high-gloss waxes or polishes.

The brick floor in the main entrance adds both visual appeal and ease of maintenance to this home. The bricks are durable, resistant to mud and water, and, like the wood stairs, deliberately not treated with a potentially slippery finish.

STRAIGHT-RUN STAIRS

Straight-run stairs, as the name suggests, go in an uninterrupted diagonal from one story to another. The simplest and often the least expensive of standard stair options, they can be as traditional as the wood hallway stairs pictured *opposite* or as contemporary as the airy open-riser flight shown *at right*.

Straight-run stairs have one major disadvantage: They take up a lot of space. Because the most comfortable angle of rise is 30 to 35 degrees, a straight staircase may take several linear feet more than other types of staircases to get from one floor to the next. This is an especially important consideration in a home with extra-high ceilings.

If space permits, however, straight-run staircases allow for tremendous design variations. They can be closed—that is, with the risers attached to the wall on at least one side—or dramatically freestanding. Possible materials range from warm-toned natural wood to high-tech metal.

Railings are important safety features. Depending on the nature of the stairs and their surroundings, you can choose gracefully turned balusters topped by a finely carved railing, or you can install a series of horizontal or vertical steel pipes.

SWITCHBACK STAIRS

Switchback stairs are really just two short, parallel, straight-run staircases connected to a midlevel landing. Switchbacks are space efficient and offer interesting possibilities for putting mid-stair space to practical use. If the landing is large enough, you can even furnish it or use it for storage.

The handsome switchback stairs pictured *below* and *at left* provide more than a compact way of getting from one point to another. They also create dramatic sculptural lines and let light from the upper-level windows stream into the ground-level seating area.

Here, the natural-wood railing has strong, simple, rectangular lines that add distinction to the center of this open-plan home. Although the woodwork has a traditional look, the floor plan reflects contemporary interest in integrating room functions and free flow of traffic from one activity center to the next. The space below the mid-level landing accommodates a convenient matching wood storage unit. Also, as the bird's-eye view *below* illustrates, the landing itself has enough room—and light—to keep plants thriving.

In this case, using switchback stairs made it possible to set the stairway in the center of the house without blocking off one section from another. Without side walls on the stairs, the whole home is open to light and interior views.

In other types of homes, such as raised ranches or bilevels, an enclosed switchback staircase might work best. Then the landing could perform a more functional job. It would provide the perfect place to store outerwear and rain gear, for example.

With modified switchbacks, two staircases meet at a landing, but are not parallel to each other. The staircases may be at right angles to each other or create a curve. For an example of a curving switchback, turn the page.

CURVING STAIRCASES

Curving staircases borrow the best features of several other types. They combine the efficient space-saving qualities of switchback and spiral staircases, the more expansive qualities of grand entrances, and the design versatility of straight-run stairs. Because the treads on these stairs may vary in size, and because they may curve unexpectedly, safe railings are particularly important.

Like most other types of stairways, curving stairs may be closed or freestanding, but—as the examples on these two pages illustrate—the freestanding versions show off the subtleties and variations of the shape especially well.

The open-riser wood-and-white stairway pictured *opposite* occupies a center-stage position between dining and living areas. Its sculptural quality integrates it into the surrounding space, and the gentle curve of the midpoint landing adds grace to what would have been an awkward interruption of open space.

The near-floor-level curve of the stairway shown *at left* turns the stairs into a focal point. The sinuous newel posts, balusters, and banisters echo the traditional decor and mellow finishes of the open-plan hallway and upstairs seating gallery.

SPIRAL STAIRCASES

Spiral staircases are romantic. They lead to the tops of castle turrets and windswept lighthouses. Spiral stairways are also very practical. They take up less square footage than almost any other type of staircase, and they are available ready-made in a variety of styles. (To learn how to install your own spiral staircase, turn to pages 128-131.) Custom-made spiral staircases provide even more design flexibility.

Many spiral staircases are true spirals—that is, three-dimensional curves with one or more complete turns around an axis. Others are not full spirals but partial ones. Although spiral staircases can be closed—indeed, ancient stone spirals were generally very narrow and bounded by walls—most modern-day metal or wood spirals are open.

Ready-built spiral stairs are usually made of metal—cast iron, steel, or aluminum—but you can also find wooden ready-mades. Wooden spiral staircases add a special decorative touch to a room, offering both the warmth of wood and the unique visual appeal and space-conservation qualities of all spiral stairs.

Special safety concerns

When you consider installing a spiral staircase, keep safety in mind. The treads on most spirals are often wedge-shaped winders or otherwise irregularly shaped, so the chances of tripping or slipping

are greater than on other types of stairs. Plan for sturdy, easy-to-grasp railings.

Choose safe surfaces for the treads. Textured metal treads reduce the chances of slipping. In other cases, wood or rubber inserts placed within the metal framework on each tread provide firm footing. Carpeting offers both visual and safety advantages. Install fitted carpet in recesses on each tread, as you would with wood or rubber, or wrap carpet around the nose of each tread to ensure a surface that's safe underfoot.

Theory into practice

The photo *above* shows the dramatic effect of a spiral stairway on the room it leads down from. Here, a circular skylight (not shown) above the stairway emphasizes the partial circle cut out of the floor and the corresponding shape of the upper railing. White-painted metal contrasts with the deep tones of the richly textured brown carpet that covers both the floor and the treads.

In the bright, open-plan home pictured *opposite,* a lightly scaled, gently winding stairway takes up little visual space—and even less floor space. As the stairs wind their way around the center post, they leave floor space free for both traffic flow and decorative accessories. Also, because the entire stairway seems to float in midair, you can see right through it from one room to the next. *(continued)*

SPIRAL STAIRCASES
(continued)

Although spiral staircases almost always are more compact than straight stairs, there's much more to them than saving space. In some cases, they can also save time and money. For example, you can buy a ready-made spiral unit for less than the cost of a pre-fabricated straight-run staircase and install it in a day or so.

Spirals also can be custom-crafted to fit both a home's decor and the unique dimensions of a given access area. The circular wood stairs shown *at right, top,* are a case in point. The owners of this home had carefully chosen the wood trim and detailing that add character to the rest of their house. To maintain the existing atmosphere, they commissioned a carpenter to custom-construct this staircase. The wood treads are decorative highlights in their own right, and the graceful ash rail is as much an architectural statement as it is a safety feature.

The owners wanted to make sure the spiral staircase was as safe and convenient as it is handsome. To achieve this, they had the stairs built with a generous 4-foot radius; in addition, the substantial 2½-inch-thick treads were spaced for an 8-inch rise. Although the treads are wedge-shaped, their width and solidity, combined with the staircase's gradual curve and slope, make for hazard-free ascents and descents.

Safe and solar

Safety was also an important factor for the owners of the dark-painted metal spiral staircase shown *opposite*. This staircase leads to a solar-heated loft that serves as a children's bedroom. Wooden triangles inserted into the framework of each tread provide a nonslip surface that harmonizes with the clear-finish wood floors in the home.

Notice, too, how the shape of the upstairs opening (see photo *at right, bottom*) makes it hard for anyone, even a running child, to fall off the stairs. The railings protect the three open sides, and the top tread's size and position let it serve as a small, safe landing as well as a top step. The gentle slope and generous curves of this staircase make it somewhat less space efficient than a more compact spiral, but still airier in appearance and less space consuming than a conventional staircase.

The open look of the staircase in this solar-heated home is as central to the home's function as it is to its appearance. The heating system relies on a free flow of hot and cool air between levels. Wooden grillwork (in the ceiling off-camera just to the right of our photo) accomplishes this; the stairway, because its landing is always open to the floor below, provides an additional channel for airflow. (See page 61 for another way a staircase can contribute to a home's energy efficiency.)

CLOSED STAIRS

By definition, a closed stairway is one in which the treads and risers attach to walls on one or both sides. The result is a fully or partially enclosed stairwell that can increase both privacy and energy efficiency.

The stairway shown *opposite* connects three levels in a home that's designed for privacy. The family consists of parents and one teenager, and the house separates their domains as much as possible. Visible at the bottom of the staircase is the daughter's bedroom. Half a flight up is the main entry, and at the top of the stairs, a study and master bedroom. The closed stairs allow family members and their guests to come and go without disturbing each other.

A closed stairway draws attention to the stairwell walls, so you'll want to choose surface materials carefully. Here the walls have the same channel cedar siding as the home's exterior, creating a gentle transition from outside to inside.

The stairway in the solar home pictured *at left* presents an attractive face and is part of the house's thermal mass. Concrete block walls and tile landings store heat from the sun during the day and release it at night. The stairwell itself, along with vents cut into the floor, let warm air from the lower floor rise to the upper story.

In this home, the stairway is a conduit for warm air, but in conventionally heated homes a fully enclosed stairway can isolate levels and separate heated from unheated areas. A straight-run enclosed stairway with a door at each end lets you close off an attic, for example, keeping furnace-heated air in the main living areas where you want it.

STYLING STAIRS

Stairways go from one level to another in bold, geometric lines—zigzags, diagonals, spirals. Those lines naturally draw the eye, so consider what design statement you want your stairway to make. A staircase can call attention to itself, play a supporting role to the stairwell walls, make a smooth transition between levels, or clearly assert passage to different domains.

On some stairways, such as the open-riser switchback shown *at right,* you feel suspended in space; as you look from one level to another, there's little interruption. In contrast, closed-tread stairs with risers and stringers often seem like extensions of the floors themselves and minimize any sense of being up in the air.

Consider which effect you prefer. Think about what your stairs do to the space they move through, and decide whether you want to reinforce or blunt that effect.

Detailing

Line draws attention to the stairway to start with, but style and detailing create the decorative mood. For example, the open-looking metal stairway pictured on this page has been softened and made somewhat more enclosed in feeling with a polished wood banister that's warm to the touch and to the eye. Treads wrapped all around with rich brown carpeting provide a quiet, cushioned climb instead of a clattery ascent—and enhance the visual effect as well.

If you prefer the more enclosed and traditional feeling of the warm-looking wood stairway *opposite,* you don't have to live in a vintage home to achieve it. The owners of this house hunted for the components of the stairway as

carefully as they did for the folk collectibles that line the wall. The pine stairway and ceiling as well as the oak flooring were transplanted from several older homes. The pine balusters and railing came from one home, the carved newel post from another.

Most vintage woodwork was harvested from mature forests and is generally of better quality than the rapidly grown lumber available today. Older homes about to be demolished, as well as architectural salvage dealers, are good sources of fine old wood for staircases.

Mixing and matching stair elements is easier than it may seem, since railing heights often are the same. Stair rails typically are 30 inches from the steps on the diagonal portion of the staircase and 34 inches high on landings. Because of this standardization, balusters from another home are likely to fit your stairway.

Keep safety in mind when placing balusters. They should be attached securely enough to catch the fall of an adult, and spaced no wider than 5 inches apart so a youngster's head cannot get caught between them.

A gallery of stairs
Stairways make fine display spots; they often offer ample wall space, and you're guaranteed an audience. Over the landing shown *opposite,* a wall-hung rug and collection of old prints brighten the view between levels and visually anchor the stairway at its midpoint. *At left,* the collection of period wood accessories adds old-time charm and leads the eye upward along the stairs' diagonal.

STAIRWAY ALTERNATIVES

Do you need to reach high places or a little-used top floor, but have no room for a full-size, conventional flight of stairs? Ladders and prefabricated folding stairs take you where you want to go, without taking up a lot of space.

The owners of the family room shown *at right* decided to turn one end of it into a library with floor-to-ceiling bookshelves. Three carpeted steps lead up to a 26-inch-high platform that conceals storage cupboards and a built-in file cabinet underneath. The platform itself is nearly 3 feet deep to accommodate the built-in bookcases and still leave room for browsers to step back and get a good look at the collection.

A wooden library ladder provides access to even the highest shelf. The top of the ladder slides along a metal rod bolted to the top of the bookcases. Wheels on the ladder's feet let it move the length of the track.

Room for one more

Three girls share the bedroom carved out of an attic pictured *opposite*. Comfortably fitting in all three took some ingenuity: The third bed was added by building it into a loft under the peak of the roof. A stairway up to the platform would have wasted too much floor space, so a ladder was chosen instead. Special hooks at the top of the ladder grip the edge of the loft to provide a secure climb. A protective polyurethane coating keeps splinters out of bare feet. For traction, sand was sprinkled on the rungs of the ladder while the polyurethane was still wet.

Both the sleeping loft and the library are used daily, so convenient out-in-the-open ladders were the most appropriate means of access. But what's the best way to get to an attic storage area that's used less frequently?

Now you see it, now you don't

Available at department stores and home improvement centers, ready-to-install folding stairways hide in the ceiling until you need them. When you have to reach the attic, a hinged wooden frame unfolds from the ceiling in two or three sections that become a full-length stairway. Most models operate manually, but you'll also find more expensive motorized units, and others that slide down from the ceiling on pulleys. All disappear from sight above a wooden trap door panel that you can cover to match or contrast decoratively with the rest of the ceiling.

Attic stairs come in standard sizes; you cut and frame a corresponding opening in the attic floor. To keep carpentry work to a minimum, try to arrange the opening to be parallel to the joists. In addition to measuring for the opening, you'll also need to measure the distance from the floor in the room below to its ceiling, and the headroom from the attic floor to the roof. When ordering stairs, be sure you have enough space in the attic to accommodate the supporting hardware and the handrail when the stairway is closed into the ceiling.

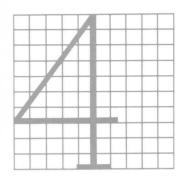

PLANNING FLOOR AND STAIR CHANGES

Once you've determined that your home needs new flooring, it's time to consider what types would be most suitable. How much traffic does the floor in question get? How is the room used, and who uses it? The answers to these questions should guide your decision about flooring. Stair changes are more complex. Unless your present stairs are irreparably hazardous or you are undertaking substantial remodeling or adding on, you probably won't make any structural changes in stairs. If you are contemplating stair changes in connection with other projects, however, you must consider location, style, materials, and safety. Let this chapter serve as a word-and-picture blueprint for planning floor and stair changes.

ANALYZING TRAFFIC AND USE PATTERNS: AN OVERVIEW

As the two-story floor plan *opposite* shows, most homes are divided into traffic and use zones, with two or more rooms or areas often belonging to one zone. If you're planning flooring changes, identify heavy-, moderate-, and light-use areas, and select flooring accordingly.

• An *entryway* or *hallway* that gets heavy traffic directly from outdoors needs durable flooring that is both easy to keep clean and not too sensitive to water or abrasives such as sand. If your hallway is right next to an entry, you might choose to match the two areas, using an attractive heavy-duty material such as quarry tile or ceramic tile.

The material you choose for a front hallway or vestibule should make a good first impression on visitors and relate well to the rest of your home. The flooring for a back entry used mostly by family members also should be attractive, of course, but you may not feel that it needs to be as much a style statement as the front entry.

Not all hallways are high-use areas. Although a main-floor hallway usually is at the very center of household activity, a second-floor hallway may get much less use. For a moderate- or light-traffic hall that serves bedrooms, you might choose a material that matches or complements the bedrooms' decor—good-quality carpeting in a color that accents their color schemes, or wood protected by several coats of polyurethane.

• *Stairways* function in much the same way as high-use hallways do. You may choose to carpet stairs for safety reasons, however, even in a home with many wood floors, area rugs, or tiled floors.

• *Stair landings* get not only up-and-down traffic but some peripheral hallway traffic as well. In the house whose plans are shown *opposite,* a stair landing also acts as a hallway into the family room/dining area. If you have an arrangement of this kind, you'll probably want to coordinate the flooring on the landing with the flooring in the adjacent room.

• *Living areas* range from active-use family rooms to quiet conversation centers. One type lends itself to rugged carpeting, spill-proof resilients, or other easily maintained materials; the other is a natural for plush carpeting, elegant area rugs, or polished wood floors.

• *Dining areas* also fall into two categories. A formal dining room is likely to receive light or moderate use. For such a room, you're probably less concerned about scuffing than about occasional spills. Wood is only one of the materials that work well in this kind of setting.

• The other type of dining area is part of a *kitchen* or the entire kitchen itself. As we discuss on pages 70 and 71, kitchens are among the most heavily used rooms. Traffic, spills, and dropped objects all threaten a kitchen floor's well-being. Resilient flooring and hard-surface tiles are probably the most practical choices.

• *Baths,* although not heavy-traffic areas, do get lots of wear and tear because they're water-use rooms. Flooring for bathrooms needs to be easily cleaned and able to stand up to spills and splashes. See pages 72 and 73 for more about bathroom floors.

• *Bedrooms* are perhaps the lightest traffic areas in most homes. In bedrooms, you can let aesthetic standards rather than durability and cleanability be your guide.

TRAFFIC AND USE ZONES

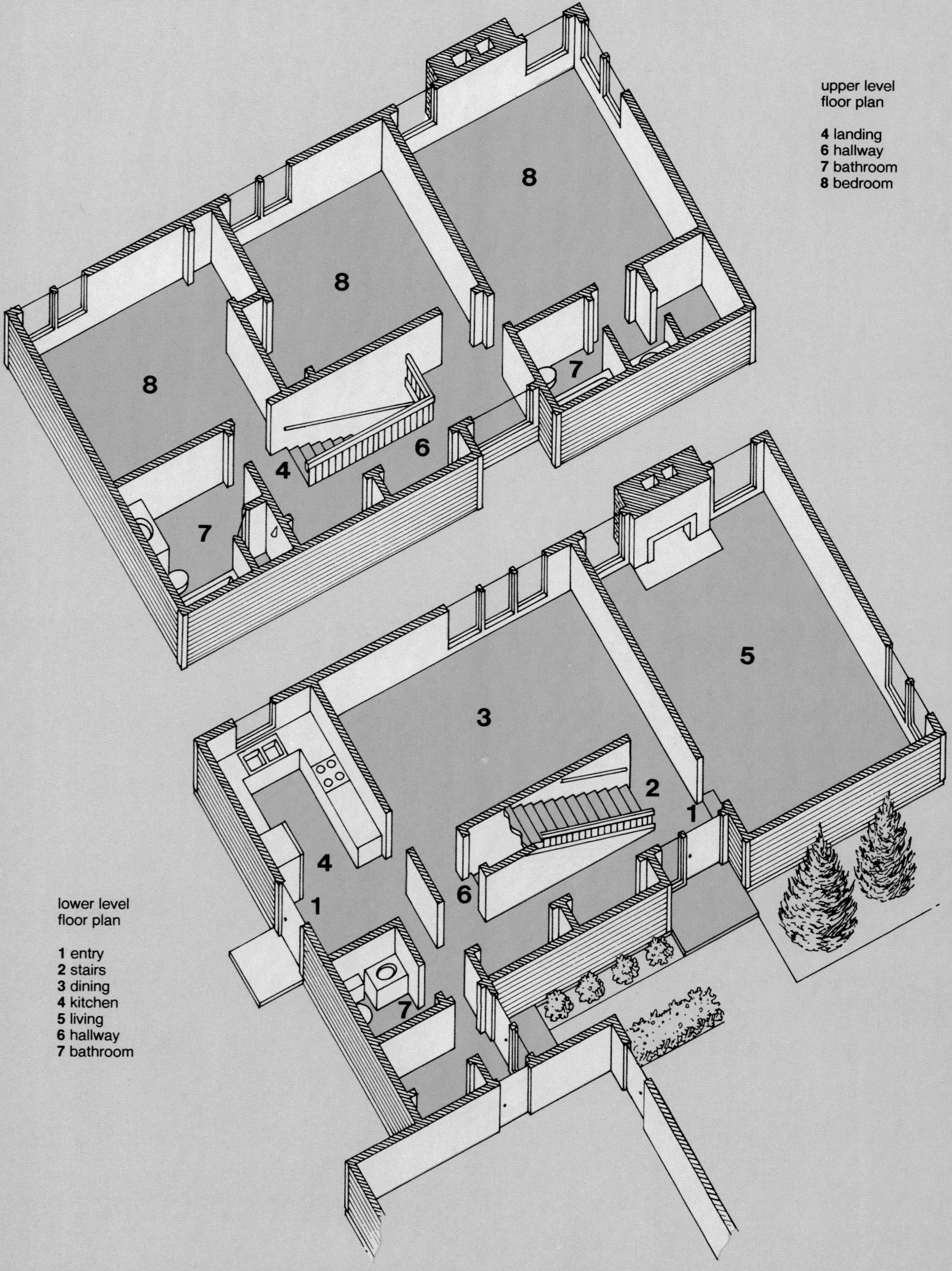

upper level
floor plan

4 landing
6 hallway
7 bathroom
8 bedroom

lower level
floor plan

1 entry
2 stairs
3 dining
4 kitchen
5 living
6 hallway
7 bathroom

ANALYZING TRAFFIC AND USE PATTERNS: TRANSITIONS

No matter how carefully you select new flooring, it won't look its best unless it works well with the flooring in adjacent and nearby rooms. Colors that are incompatible, textures that compete, a great new floor that is next door to a battered old one— all represent the wasted effort of an unrealized decorating opportunity.

There's also a more subtle aspect to consider when planning flooring transitions— dealing with different materials within a single space. The tile-and-carpet floor design in the open-plan living area pictured *below* illustrates this approach.

Here, tile beneath the wood-burning stove does more than provide fire safety. It also emphasizes the shape of the angled wall that partially separates the sitting and dining areas and helps visually link the carpeted area with the tiled kitchen.

Note that the entry hall and stairs pictured *opposite, lower right* carry this same flooring design through to another zone in the same home. Here tile serves in the entry, with carpet on the stairs. You might also use a tile border around the perimeter of a carpeted room that receives a lot of through traffic, creating what

amounts to a hallway around softer flooring material.

The two-zone bath shown *opposite, upper left* illustrates a more private transitional zone. Here carpet makes the grooming area an ideal "barefoot" room; ceramic tiles in the inner part of the bath make for flooring that cleans very easily and that can stand up to moisture.

The master bedroom/master bath combination pictured *opposite, upper right* carries out a similar division of function. Carpeting in the bedroom provides both decorative focus and comfort underfoot. The tiled bath floor is durable and

easy to maintain. Keep in mind that bedrooms and baths are to some extent barefoot rooms; for that reason you will probably want a soft bath mat in a tiled bath, and perhaps a bedside area rug in a quarry-tiled or wood-floored bedroom.

Sometimes transition is as much a matter of architectural interest as of function. The two softly carpeted steps leading up from the living room in the foreground of the photo *opposite, lower left* give the room an almost sculptural quality. Carpet on both levels contrasts subtly with the tile in the T-shape "hallway."

DUAL-PURPOSE TRANSITIONS

BATH TRANSITIONS

STAIRS AND LANDINGS

PLANNING KITCHEN FLOOR SURFACES

ONE FLOOR THREE WAYS

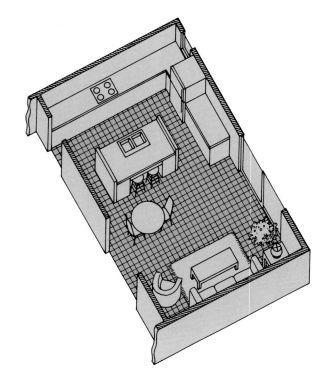

Kitchens come in a wide range of sizes, shapes, and styles, but almost all have several traits in common. They are busy places, often central to family activity—and they are potentially messy places as well. The neatest, most conscientious cook can't avoid an occasional spill or spatter. And depending upon the age and nature of family members, the kitchen floor also must withstand an onslaught of cracker crumbs, scuff marks, toy car traffic, and more.

In addition to having to hold up under steady, hard use, a kitchen floor should be comfortable to stand on; if the main part of the floor is a non-resilient material, you might place a small braided rug or cushioned mat at the main

work areas, particularly near the sink area.

Even if your kitchen is not one of the larger rooms in your home, it is one of the most important. Family members and probably guests, too, spend a good deal of time there. Because the floor usually is the largest uninterrupted surface in the kitchen, the material you choose will go a long way toward establishing a decorating tone for the entire room.

All kitchens need flooring that's durable and fairly skidproof. The precise material you select, however, depends on how much money you plan to spend on the flooring, how large the room is—on a small scale, for example, some flooring works better than others, and the reverse is true as well—and how the kitchen

relates visually to other parts of your home. Here's a brief rundown on the materials that are most commonly used in kitchens. For more about these and other flooring materials, see chapters 5 and 6.

• *Resilient flooring* is nearly impervious to any kind of dirt; it's ideal for kitchens where easy maintenance is a high priority, and it provides good looks at moderate cost.

• *Hard-surface materials* include quarry tile, ceramic tile, and slate. These materials are durable and perform admirably in kitchens with direct access to the outdoors. In fact, if you'd like to create a visual link to an adjacent patio, matching hard-surface materials indoors and out is a good way to do it.

• *Wood* may seem at first like a less-than-practical flooring

for a kitchen. If protected with several layers of polyurethane, however, wood can stand up to normal kitchen activities and provide a decorative link to other wood floors in your home. The island-accented kitchen pictured *above, left* shows that a wood floor can be compatible with contemporary styling. (Of course, wood floors work well with more traditional fixtures, too.) Here, the same diagonal strips were used on one wall.

• *Carpeting* provides a very comfortable surface for cooks who are on their feet a lot. Its sound-absorbing qualities are an advantage, too. A factor to consider, however, is that keeping carpeting clean in the kitchen is more difficult than maintaining other types of flooring in the same area.

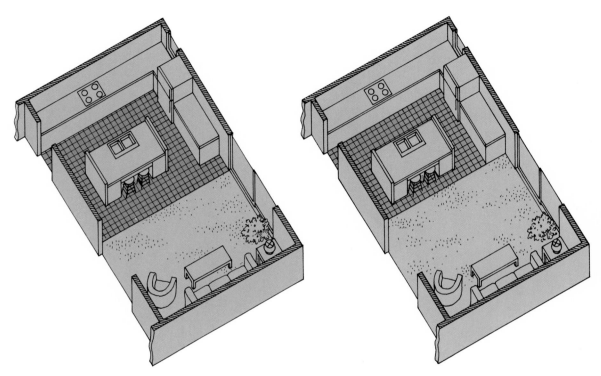

Exploring the possibilities

The kitchen illustrated in the floor plans *opposite* and *above* features a sink/breakfast-bar island. It's an open-plan kitchen that blends into the adjacent family room. Sliding glass doors, which mark the transition from kitchen to family room, open directly onto a patio. The three floor plans shown here illustrate a variety of flooring treatments. Each is suitable not only for a kitchen/family room combination like this, but also for any kitchen with more than one activity zone.

The first alternative shown here uses the same material throughout. Here, the choice is quarry tile, for continuity with the surface of the adjacent patio. Quarry tile, however, is fairly expensive. A less costly combination of materials may be necessary to fit your budget. You might use quarry tile in a more limited area. Or you might decide to use more economical materials throughout the space. In the second plan, highly durable vinyl tile that looks like quarry tile is used in the kitchen. Color-coordinated carpeting marks the family room.

The third plan shows an even more limited use of moisture- and spill-proof material. Depending on your budget, you could use either quarry tile or resilient flooring underneath all areas where spills are likely. Here, that means extending it far enough beyond the breakfast bar to allow the bar stools to rest on it; carpeting goes the rest of the way.

If your kitchen opens to a formal living area, or if you use your family room more for adult entertaining than for children's play, you might also consider using wood in a layout like this.

The illustration *at right* shows how hard-surface tile or resilient flooring, when used as *coving,* provides a handsomely finished look for your new floor. Coving also makes cleaning simpler, since there are no cracks between counters and flooring for dirt to nestle in. For a more economical alternative that goes well with virtually any resilient flooring, consider black vinyl coving; it blends into the background and gives the cabinets a tidy, unobtrusive base.

PLANNING BATH FLOOR SURFACES

THREE BATHS, THREE OPTIONS

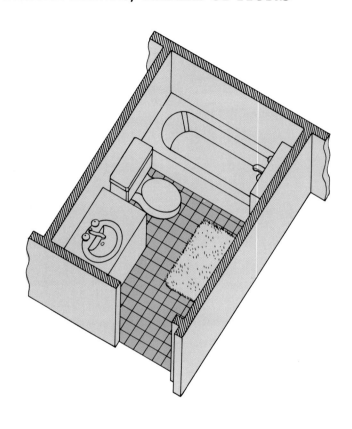

Once upon a time, many bathroom floors were a standard combination of small black and white tiles, often very attractive but without much scope for the imagination. Now bathroom floors come in many designs and colors, all in materials that are slip-resistant, durable, comfortable underfoot, and easy to clean. The material or materials you select from the many available depend, as kitchen flooring does, on cost and use.

• All *resilient flooring* can take heavy wear, but sheet flooring holds up much better under moisture than vinyl tiles do. Water may seep into the spaces between the tiles and eventually cause the adhesive to loosen.

• *Ceramic tile*, though more expensive to buy and install than other options, offers the ideal combination of durability and good looks. Keep in mind that with both resilient and ceramic flooring, you'll want a bath mat or a washable area rug to put on the floor near the tub or shower.

The brown ceramic tile used in the bathroom pictured *above, left* has an added advantage. It absorbs and retains heat from the sun's rays, which shine in through the angled skylight.

• *Carpeting* is ideal under bare feet, but it holds up best in less-traveled areas such as a master bath or a powder room. It's usually not a practical choice for the main bath or one used by children.

Exploring the possibilities

A typical 5x8-foot bath, like the one shown in the first floor plan, offers little room for experimentation. Because of limited floor space, it's usually not practical to combine permanent flooring treatments, although small mats or rugs can provide some visual variety and comfort underfoot. The rug pictured in this floor plan tops a ceramic tile floor; it easily can be moved closer to the tub for use as a bath mat.

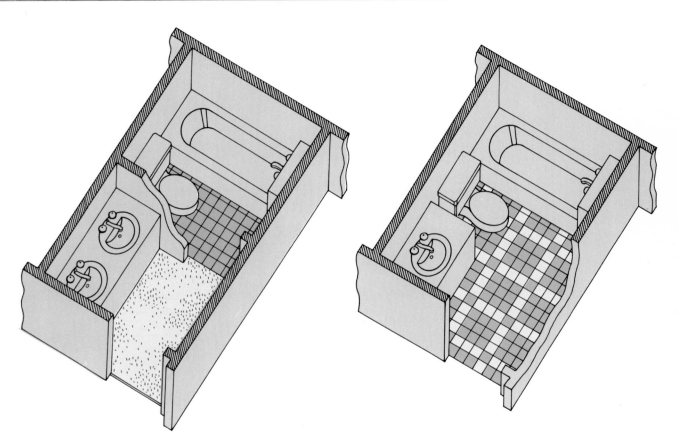

Larger baths are another story. If the dimensions permit, you can use more than one material to great advantage. Compartmentalized baths in particular lend themselves to multiflooring treatments. These really are little rooms within rooms, with a partition separating a vanity and dressing room, for example, from the tub and toilet. A layout like the left one shown on this page is typical. Here, a soft surface—cut-to-measure carpeting, in this case—covers the vanity area floor; hard-surface material is reserved for the floor near the toilet and, especially, the tub, where water tolerance is particularly important.

Although ceramic tile or resilient flooring can be cold to walk on barefoot, they do give you the opportunity to build visual appeal into the floor without using a second material. The bathroom illustrated in the third floor plan shows one way to do this. Here, a dark background is punctuated and

made much more interesting with a large check design of tiles in a lighter shade of the same color.

Coving, as shown in the drawing *at right,* is a good way to ease maintenance chores in the bath as well as in the kitchen. You can use ceramic or resilient materials, in matching or complementary colors. You might, for example, consider matching the coving to either the wall or the floor tiles.

PLANNING
STAIR CHANGES

Changing a stairway, or adding a new one, isn't easy. First of all, any stairway eats up a considerable amount of floor space. In a home with 8-foot ceilings, for example, a safe, code-approved straight-run staircase would need a minimum of 300 square feet. Then you have to multiply that number by two, since the new stairs would affect two levels. What's more, you have to allow space at the top and bottom—at least 12½ square feet in total—for access to the stairs.

Square footage isn't the only consideration, either. Any stairway, especially a main staircase, determines traffic patterns on both of the levels it serves. This means you have to think about not only where a stairway starts out, but also where it ends up, a three-dimensional proposition that architects call "vertical circulation."

Let's begin by considering how you can improve vertical circulation with alternatives to the conventional straight-run staircase. Then we'll look at how you might add an ordinary stairway—to a basement, for example, or an about-to-be-finished upper level. Finally, on pages 76 and 77, we'll show how landings can help stairs begin and end where you want them to.

Alternative stairways
If you simply can't envision giving up more than 600 square feet of floor space to an ordinary staircase, consider these other, more compact ways to get up and down.
• *Circular stairways.* A circular stairway can occupy as little as 32 square feet (16 on each level), and because you can look right through most circular units, they seem to take up even less space than they

actually do. Prefab circular stairs are easy to install, too. (To learn how, see pages 128-131.) However, circular stairways pose a couple of problems: Moving large furniture up and down one is difficult, and you can easily stumble on the wedge-shaped treads.
• *Ship's ladders.* To envision this one, imagine a stepladder permanently fixed at top and bottom. Ship's ladders rise at a 50- to 75-degree angle, a much more rapid rate than ordinary staircases. They have shallower treads and higher risers, too, thus further conserving space. You wouldn't want one between main levels in a home, but for secondary vertical circulation—to an attic or loft bed, for example—a ship's ladder might be just what the captain ordered.
• *Disappearing stairways.* These units fold down from a ceiling, scissors-fashion, to provide access to an attic. Like spiral stairs, wood or metal disappearing stairways are available in kit form. More about these on page 65.

Adding a stairway
Finding space for an entirely new stairway takes imagination. Maybe you can sacrifice a closet or give up 3 feet or so along one end of a room. Or maybe the stairway you need doesn't have to be inside your home at all. The illustration *at right* shows how you could gain *exterior* access to a basement by excavating down to its footing, installing stairs, and protecting everything from the weather with bulkhead doors.

If you really can't get by with anything but a new interior staircase, study the plans in the box *opposite,* then turn the page to learn how landings can help you get where you want to go.

ANATOMY OF A
BULKHEAD STAIRWAY

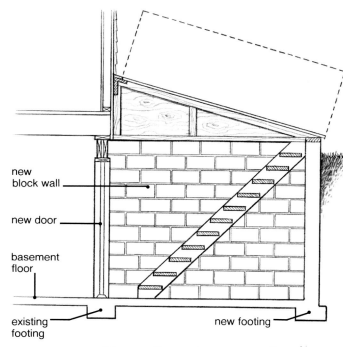

new block wall

new door

basement floor

existing footing

new footing

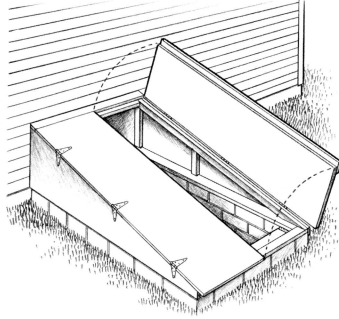

FINDING SPACE FOR AN INTERIOR STAIRWAY

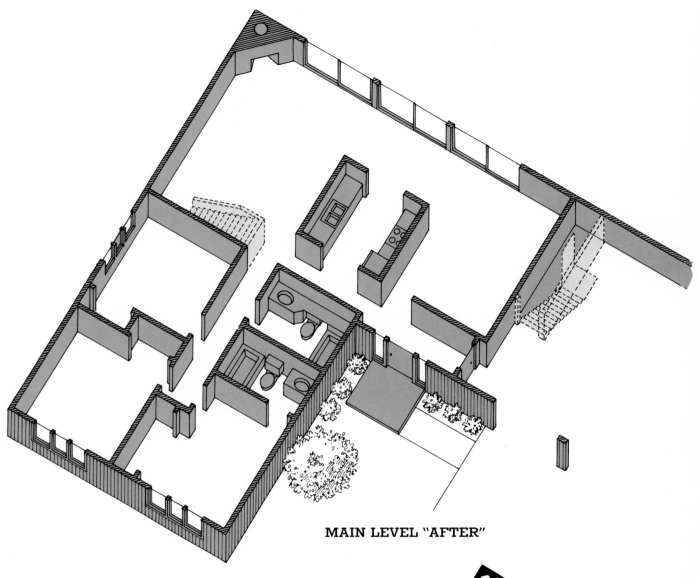

MAIN LEVEL "AFTER"

Before you choose a location for a new stairway, think about how traffic now moves through your home and how the new stairs would change circulation patterns. Would you like to get upstairs directly from a main entry, or to the basement from a spot near the kitchen or garage? Do you have other remodeling plans that might include a new stairway?

In general, look for locations that won't affect plumbing and heating runs and that don't call for removing a load-bearing wall. Also, consult codes for minimum widths, headroom, and rise-to-run ratios (see pages 82 and 83).

The plan *above* shows two possible locations for a new stairway in a typical ranch-style home. One, which would best serve a new or unfinished upper level, occupies space at one end of a family room. Because this one goes up, it begins near an exterior wall and ascends toward the house's center, where headroom upstairs is adequate.

The other stairway, at the right of the plan, was created by partitioning off part of an attached garage. As shown, this stairway would provide access to a basement; if run up, it could lead to new rooms above the garage. *(continued)*

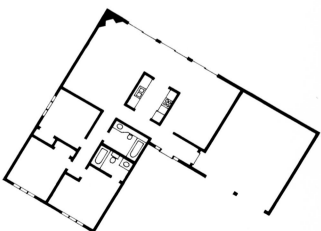

MAIN LEVEL "BEFORE"

PLANNING
STAIR CHANGES
(continued)

A LANDING AT THE BOTTOM

Looking for a way to reduce the space a stairway occupies or a means of improving access to stairs? A landing might be the answer.

Where you position a landing depends on what you want it to do. The drawings on these pages illustrate your four main landing options.

In the example shown here, a landing at the bottom gets you around a dead-end situation; without a landing here the stairs would be too steep for safety, or they'd run smack into a wall.

Also known as platform, dogleg, or L-type stairs, this configuration essentially turns the bottom two or three steps sideways. If you'd like a stairway that's accessible from

both sides, simply include a second set of bottom steps.

How big must a bottom landing be? At a minimum, it should measure, in both directions, the width of the stairs. In other words, a stairway that's 36 inches wide should have a 36x36-inch landing. Increase the landing's length if a door—to a closet or the outdoors, for example—opens onto it. You shouldn't have to stand on a step to open the door.

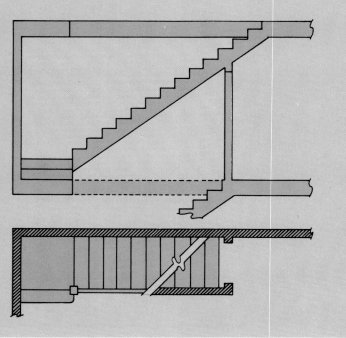

A LANDING IN THE MIDDLE

A landing at or near the middle of a stair run greatly reduces the length of the opening between levels, but it needs a correspondingly wider stairwell. In the example shown here, known

as a U-type or switchback stairway, the opening must be slightly more than twice as wide as it would be for a straight-run stair.

Stairs with a landing in the middle need not return on

themselves. If your home's layout permits, its stairway could ascend to an intermediate landing, then turn 90 degrees to the left or right.

Stairs with a landing in the middle work especially well

in split-entry homes, where the landing can serve as an entry platform. Extraordinarily long straight-run stairs, such as you might have outdoors, can also benefit from a landing at or near the middle. In commercial buildings with very high ceilings, for example, codes typically limit a flight of interior stairs to 16 steps. A landing at that point allows you to pause and catch your breath before continuing your ascent.

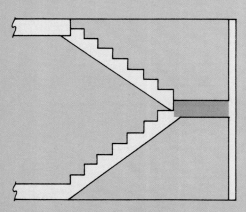

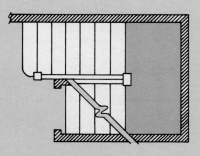

A LANDING AT THE TOP

Like a landing at the bottom, a landing at the top can save space and get you around an awkward situation. Most of the considerations for a landing at the bottom also apply to one at the top: The platform must be at least as wide and as long as the stairs are wide; the platform must be larger if a door swings onto it; and the platform can be accessible from either or both directions.

In addition, you also have to consider what's going on *underneath* a stairway with a landing at the top. If there's another set of stairs—to a basement, for example—headroom must be at least 78 inches, or that stairway also will need a landing at

the top. This can be a problem, because most codes require that basement and main living areas be separated by a door at the top of the stairs and that the door must not swing over a landing lower than the level of the main floor.

What all of this adds up to is that if your home has 8-foot-high ceilings and staircases one atop the other, don't count on providing more than two steps between a top-of-the-stair landing and the upper level. If there's no stairway below, and you need more steps, consider building a closet down there.

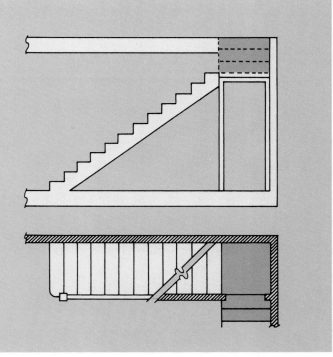

LANDINGS AT TOP AND BOTTOM

Sometimes called a double-L, this configuration suits a situation where you need turnings both below and above, as you might where headroom upstairs is limited by a sloping ceiling.

Double-L stairs present all the same design limitations as top- and bottom-landing versions, times two. Also, you might be surprised to learn that a stairway with landings top and bottom is typically a foot or so *longer* than a comparable single-L staircase; the second landing eats up a disproportionate amount of space.

One way to reduce the length of a double-L stairway is to elongate the leg of one L, preferably the one at the

bottom. Another is to switch to a U configuration like the one shown on the bottom of the opposite page.

All of the stair designs illustrated on these pages can be made up with standard millwork components—landings and all. To learn about what's involved in assembling a staircase with prefabricated components, see pages 124-127.

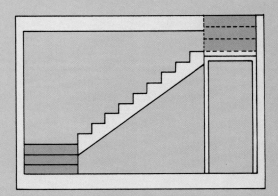

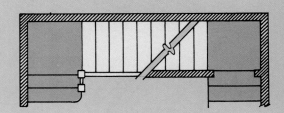

IF YOU'RE PLANNING AN ADDITION

If you're thinking about adding on to your home, one of your first decisions—after you know where the addition will go—is how it will relate to the level of the floor or floors in the existing house. Do you want new and old floors to flow together in a single, unbroken plane, or would you rather step up or down to the new space?

You need to make this decision early on in your planning because, with changes in level, a difference of an inch or two is considerably worse than a change of a foot or two. A room that's only slightly higher or lower than the one next to it presents a tripping hazard—and if you want new and old floors to come out even, you have to account for that before beginning to excavate.

The anatomy drawing below shows the underpinnings for a typical main-level addition over a crawl space. Everything rests on concrete *footings* that are below the frost line. Atop them is a wood or masonry *foundation.* If the new room will be more than 10 to 12 feet wide, you'll also need a wood or steel *girder* down the center. On top of this substructure goes a *sill,* then joists, subflooring, and finish flooring.

A contractor, in determining how deep to dig for an addition, works from the top down. The thicknesses of subflooring, joists, sills, blocks, footings, and even the mortar joints between blocks are uniformly dimensioned, but your contractor will also have to know how thick your finish flooring will be. If you plan to continue the same flooring material— tiling, for instance—out into the new space, the contractor can simply establish the elevation of existing subflooring as the benchmark. If you plan to use a different material, however, the contractor will need to adjust all measurements accordingly. *(continued)*

ANATOMY OF A FOUNDATION

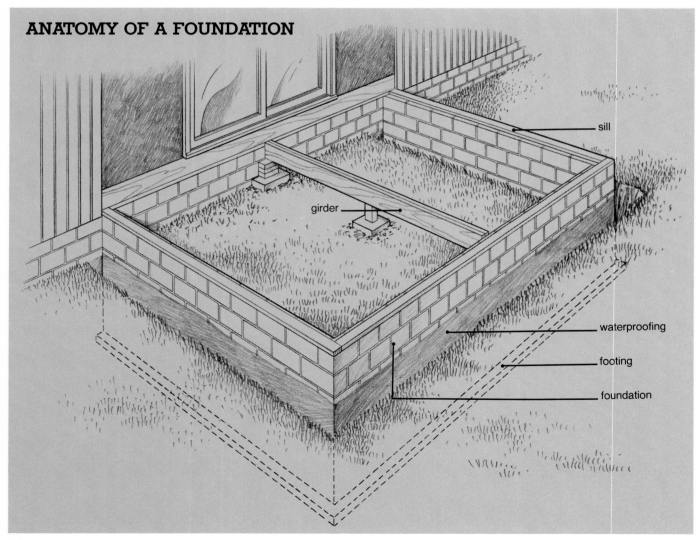

sill

girder

waterproofing

footing

foundation

TYING TOGETHER OLD AND NEW FLOORS

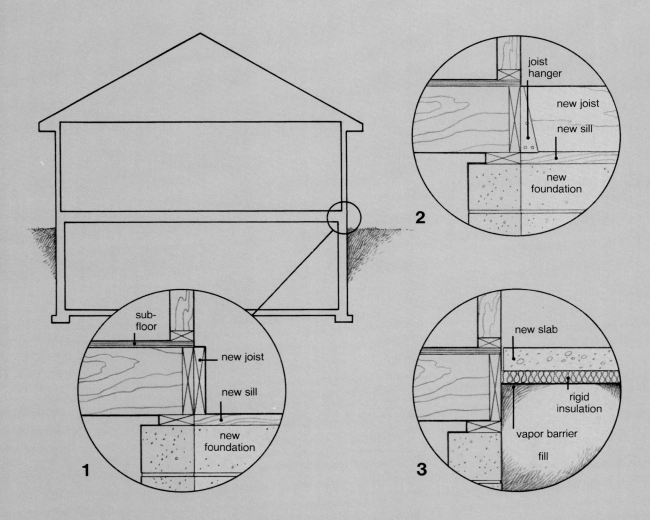

Details in the drawing above show three ways the floor for an addition might attach to the existing house. All presuppose that the same finish flooring will be used in new and old spaces.
• *Detail 1* illustrates what carpenters will do if joists for the new space will run parallel to the house, as they would over the foundation shown on the opposite page. Here a new joist is simply bolted or nailed to an existing joist. Ends of this joist, and of others that will run parallel to it, will rest atop the new sill and be tied together with headers.
• *Detail 2* depicts the situation if joists for the addition will run perpendicular to the house. In this case, *joist hangers* will be nailed or bolted to an existing joist, then ends of the new joists will fit into the hangers.
• *Detail 3* shows a different method of construction—a concrete slab under the addition. For a slab, the contractor excavates to below the frost line and adds slag, gravel, or crushed-stone *fill*. Over the fill goes a polyethylene *vapor barrier*, then *rigid insulation*. Finally, the contractor pours a concrete slab that will serve as the new subfloor.

IF YOU'RE PLANNING AN ADDITION
(continued)

PLANNING A STEP-DOWN ADDITION

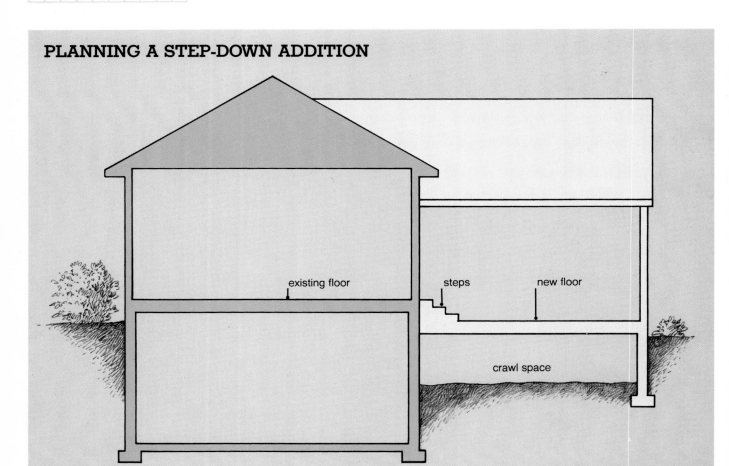

existing floor

steps

new floor

crawl space

No law says the floor in an addition has to be at the same height as the floors in the rest of your home. In fact, lots can be said for a new room that's at least a few feet *lower* than the house it's attached to. Here are three good reasons for a step-down addition.

• Sloping terrain would require costly foundation work to bring the new room up to main-floor level. Foundations can be unsightly, too.

• A sizable addition might dwarf your home. This especially applies to single-level houses. Lowering the floor lets you also lower the addition's roof, creating a harmonious difference in scale between new and old parts of the house.

• Inside, you want to clearly differentiate between added and existing spaces. Walls can do this, of course, but a change in levels can visually set apart a new family room, for example, yet keep it in touch with adjacent rooms. Lowering the floor also offers an opportunity to raise the ceiling and make the new room more dramatic.

Ground rules
The cutaway drawing *above* shows a typical step-down addition at the back of a single-level ranch house. Originally, the back door was four steps above grade. The floor of the new wing, built over a crawl space, drops three steps below main-floor level, which greatly improves access to the backyard. The addition's roof is commensurately lower, too.

In a home with a walk-out basement, the difference in elevation between existing and added-on space could be even greater, up to about half the height of the basement ceiling. A second half-flight of interior stairs might then lead from the addition to the basement.

Note that in this drawing steps to the addition are in the new room. Incorporating a stairway into the existing house would require major structural surgery, and probably extensive reshuffling of space as well.

ADDING UP

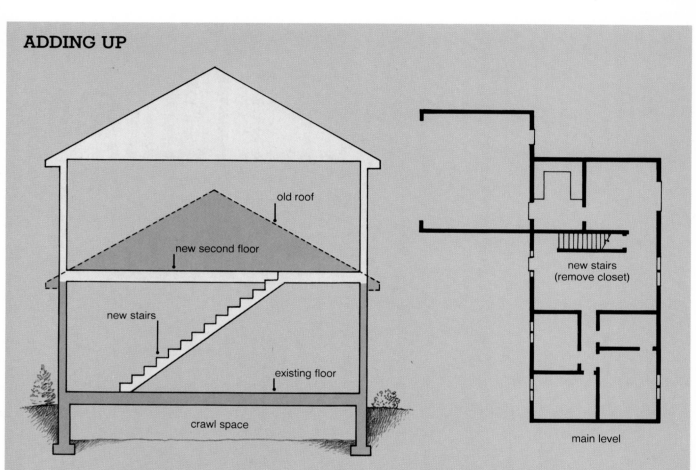

old roof

new second floor

new stairs

existing floor

crawl space

new stairs
(remove closet)

main level

If site or zoning restrictions rule out extending the main level of your home or building a step-down addition, maybe you can add *up.* Be warned, however, that building a full or partial new floor on top of a house poses a series of structural and design challenges: You have to remove the old roof and possibly beef up the lower story to support the weight of the addition. Also, you have to keep the new room or rooms from making your house look top-heavy. And you have to figure out how you're going to get up to the new space. Let's examine these factors one at a time.

• *Structural considerations* should be carefully assessed by an architect, engineer, or qualified contractor. Generally, if your home's ceiling joists are 2x8s or bigger and spaced no more than 16 inches apart, they're strong enough to support another floor. If not, you'll need to add more joists or reinforce existing joists by nailing a second member to each. You may also need to add girders or support columns on the main level.

• *To minimize the bulk of a second-floor addition,* you might be able to retain the front slope of your present roof and build a full-width dormer at the back. If not, consult with an architect or house designer, who can plan a roof shape, window locations, and materials choices that will make the new story look as if it's always been there.

• *Where you place a stairway* affects traffic patterns throughout your house. Don't count on using an existing attic stairway. It's probably too steep and also may be too narrow to suit code requirements for a primary staircase. If you already have stairs to a basement, consider building the new stairs directly over them. If not, you might have to sacrifice a closet downstairs (see the plan above) or steal space from a main-floor room. Pages 74-77 present additional possibilities for incorporating a stairway.

STAIR PLANNING BASICS

Whether building a new stairway on site or ordering a prefabricated one, you need to consider three crucial design factors: headroom, stairway width, and slope. The drawings *at right* illustrate general planning guidelines; check local building codes for specific requirements. (Here we focus on straight-run stairs, but the same basic principles apply to more complicated types.)

• *Headroom.* Observe how you ascend or descend a staircase and you'll notice that you rise on the balls of your feet and move with a slight bounce. This means that for safety, overhead clearance must be slightly greater than the height of a "typically" tall person. Most building codes require a minimum headroom of 78 inches for service stairways and at least 80 inches for stairways in a home's main living areas. Headroom is measured from the *nosing line,* an imaginary line connecting the front edges of the treads to the lowest point of the overhead ceiling. If you can provide more than the minimum headroom, you'll find it easier to move furniture.

• *Stairway width.* Building codes typically dictate a minimum width of 30 inches for service stairways and 3 feet for main stairways, but wider dimensions are more comfortable and allow two people to pass each other more easily.

• *Slope.* An incline of 30 to 35 degrees ensures comfortable climbs and safe descents. The exact angle of a stairway depends on the ratio of the height of the risers to the depth of the treads. Before calculating this ratio, examine the drawing *at lower right* to familiarize yourself with the vocabulary of stairway geometry.

HEADROOM

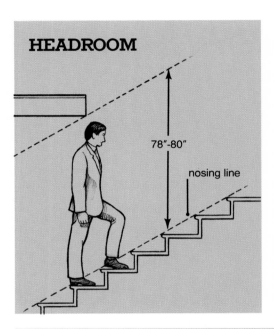

78"-80"

nosing line

STAIRWAY WIDTH

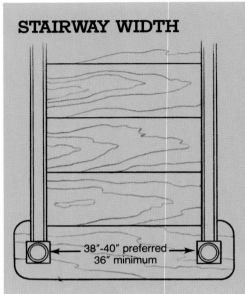

38"-40" preferred
36" minimum

STAIRWAY GEOMETRY

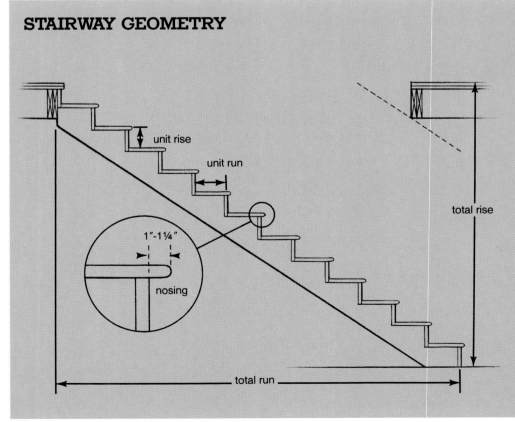

unit rise

unit run

1"-1¼"

nosing

total rise

total run

FIGURING RISE AND RUN

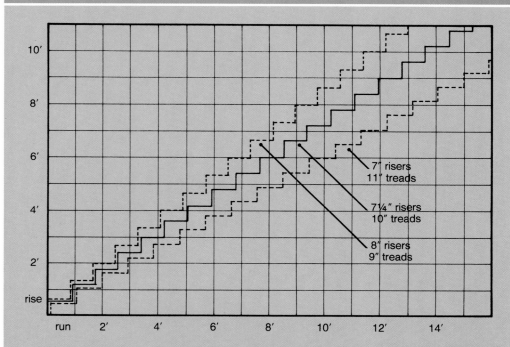

7″ risers
11″ treads

7¼″ risers
10″ treads

8″ risers
9″ treads

10′

8′

6′

4′

2′

rise

run   2′   4′   6′   8′   10′   12′   14′

Use this chart to estimate approximately how much space a safe, comfortable stairway would take up. The upper line represents the maximum slope; the lower, the minimum. First, determine the total vertical rise.

Next, read along the horizontal and vertical axes for the total amount of run available. If the horizontal and vertical axes intersect between the two straight lines, you can fit a straight-run staircase into the space

available; if not, you may be able to include a landing or landings, as explained on pages 76 and 77. For exact calculations, use the formula given below.

floor to the upper finished floor. An 8-foot ceiling, for example, plus 9 inches for joists and other materials between the ceiling and the floor above would bring the total rise to 105 inches. Because residential stairways typically have between 13 and 16 steps, try dividing the total run by whole numbers from 13 to 16 until the result is between 7 and 7¾ inches, an acceptable riser height. In our example, dividing the total rise by 14 steps gives a riser height of 7½ inches. To find a suitable tread depth, use the formula unit rise + unit run = 17 to 18. In this case, tread depth can range between 9½ and 10½ inches; for our example we'll select a tread depth of 10 inches. To calculate the total run of the staircase, multiply the number of treads by their depth. Keeping in mind that there is always one fewer tread than risers, multiply 13 x 10, for a total run of 130 inches.

How much do you need to know?

If you are ordering prefabricated stairs, some manufacturers will send a representative to your home to take measurements. In other cases, you'll have to order the staircase yourself and provide the correct specifications. You'll need to tell the manufacturer the stairway width, the total rise, and an estimated total run. Depending on what stock is available, the actual run may differ slightly from your estimate, but you'll have a close approximation of where the bottom of the staircase will be. If you're building your own staircase, you'll have to take all measurements and make all calculations, but the resulting stairway will be the exact dimensions you prefer.

As shown on the drawing *opposite,* the *total rise* is the distance from the top of the finish floor on the lower level to the top of the finish floor on the upper level. The *total run* is the horizontal distance taken up by the staircase. *Unit rise* is the vertical distance from the top of one tread to the top of the tread above it. *Unit run* is the horizontal distance from the back edge of one tread to the back edge of the next tread. Because the top floor becomes the final tread of the

staircase, stairways always have one fewer unit run than unit rise.

Most building codes also require that each tread overhang the riser beneath it to provide extra toe room. *Nosing* should project 1 to 1¼ inches on closed tread stairways, but only ½ inch on open-tread staircases. (Note: Nosing is omitted when figuring unit run.)

Riser heights of 7 to 7¾ inches, combined with tread depths of 9½ to 11½ inches, result in safe, comfortable

stairways. Keep in mind, too, that a straight run of stairs should have no more than 16 steps without a landing.

Armed with these specifications and a pocket calculator, you're ready to determine the combination that will work for your new staircase. The following formula will help you establish the ratio: unit rise + unit run = 17 to 18 inches.

A step-by-step example
Start by measuring the distance from the lower finished

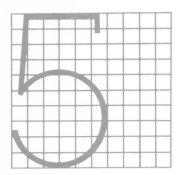

CHOOSING AND BUYING SOFT FLOOR COVERINGS

Pay a visit to any good-size flooring store and you'll find a mind-boggling wealth of soft floor coverings available today. The selection is so wide that it's difficult to pick colors and patterns—let alone know which products will wear the best and resist soil longest. That's where this chapter will help. Here you'll find the basic information you need about buying carpet, area rugs, and resilient flooring. Combine this background information with sound advice from a knowledge-able flooring dealer in your area, and you'll be able to shop for floor coverings with skill and confidence.

CARPET

Carpet represents a sizable investment, so it pays to do your homework before you begin to shop. You'll save time in the long run, and also be better able to judge quality.

To help pinpoint your needs, first ask yourself where you plan to install the carpet. Think carefully about soil and traffic conditions. Be realistic about how much upkeep you will give your carpet. Are you willing to vacuum daily, or just once a week? Keep in mind, too, what look you prefer. Your answers will help you determine how much to spend, the level of quality to look for, and your color, texture, and fiber choices.

Choosing colors

Color selection should be fun, but it should be sensible, too. Choose a color that you like, of course, but make sure it also works well in your home, and in the specific setting you've chosen for it.

When you shop for carpet, take along color guides such as fabric swatches and paint chips. Even better, see if you can take a carpet swatch home to judge the color in your own surroundings. Or use the "shop at home" service offered by some retailers so you can see carpets under your own lighting conditions and with your furnishings.

Consider where the carpet is going to go. Don't immediately assume you need the darkest possible shade in a high-use area. Although dark colors do hide dirt, lint and dusty footprints often stand out. A carpet that's a solid medium shade or a blend of related colors will show tracks and soil the least, making it a practical selection for heavy-traffic areas such as family rooms or entryways.

Texture in depth

When you shop for carpet, you'll find a range of textures. Texture is partly determined by whether the pile—the surface of the carpet that you see and walk on—is looped (uncut), sheared (cut), or a combination of the two. The height of the pile affects texture, too.
● *Looped pile* may be one level or multilevel (with high and low loops). Short, dense, one-level looped carpet holds up especially well under hard use. Soil and spills tend to stay on the surface, making it a practical choice for kitchens.
● *Cut pile* offers several options, which differ in the amount of twist in the yarn used to make up the pile. You can choose a smooth, velvety texture—known as plush—with almost no twist or a number of twisted-yarn variations. There are also cut-and-loop textures in either multilevel or level pile.
● One of the best-known twisted-yarn carpets is *saxony,* with a moderate twist; tightly twisted *frieze* is another possibility. These are found in cut versions only.
● *Shag* consists of long pile, either cut or uncut. Shag requires frequent vacuuming to look its best.
● *Cut-and-loop combinations* are available in one- or multi-level piles. One-level combinations are known as *random shears*.

Most plushes show some "shading" when walked on. This is not a defect, but a natural characteristic of cut-pile fabrics. Textures such as twists and loops, or those that have a definite "pattern," are less likely to show signs of traffic than soft plushes are.

(continued)

CARPET
(continued)

Most carpet produced today is manufactured in one of four ways. The most popular and widely used method is *tufting*. In the tufting process, pile yarns are stitched into a backing fabric. The primary backing, which the surface yarns are secured to, may be made of jute or, more likely today, of a woven polypropylene. Then a secondary backing of jute or a synthetic material is laminated to the first for additional strength and stability.

Woven carpets get their names, such as Wilton and Axminster, from the particular looms they're produced on. Each loom creates a distinctive finish, but all weave pile, weft, and warp yarns (see page 91) into a solid fabric.

Hundreds of barbed needles interlock a mat of fibers with a prewoven fabric core to form a *needle-punched* carpet. This type of carpet works well both indoors and out, and resists damage from water, insects, mold, and sun.

Oriental carpets and rugs are *hand-knotted,* a laborious process of wrapping individual pile yarns around a woven core. (For more information about hand-knotted carpets, turn to page 91.)

One of the most important qualities to look for in any type of carpet is *density*. Dense carpets, with closely packed surface yarns and closely woven backing, wear best and look better longer.

One test for density is to bend a piece of the carpet backward. If it ''grins'' (that is, shows a lot of backing through the pile), it's best to look for a higher-quality carpet.

You'll also come across the terms *denier* and *ply*. Denier describes the fiber size and weight; ply tells how many strands are twisted together to form the yarn. High denier and ply figures indicate a high-quality carpet.

Fiber considerations
In addition to density, the *fiber content* of a carpet's pile will help determine how the carpet will perform. Both natural and synthetic fibers are used (see chart *opposite*) and quality-conscious carpet manufacturers choose fibers to take advantage of the fibers' best features and minimize their shortcomings. Fibers called ''fourth-'' or ''new-generation'' offer antistatic properties and resist soil and stains.

Problems with static electricity most often occur under dry, cold conditions. To help prevent static buildup, choose fibers such as olefin and polyester that have naturally low static generation, or ones that have been treated to guard against producing static, such as fourth-generation nylons.

Carpets can be made to resist soil and stains by the use of modified fibers, by treatments applied during manufacturing, or by treatments applied after the carpet is made. Also available are products to spray on already-installed carpets. These products usually don't last as long as those incorporated into the carpet fiber. You can also purchase carpets that have undergone antimicrobial treatment to retard the growth of bacteria and fungi and prevent the odors they cause.

Carpet padding
To prolong the good looks of your new carpet, invest in good padding. This cushion absorbs shocks, creates a more comfortable surface, and helps insulate the floor.
- *Felt padding* may be made entirely of animal hair or a combination of hair and other fibers. Animal hair provides excellent insulation and long service, but can be expensive. A blend is more economical, but not as effective or long lasting as all-hair padding. Some felt paddings have a rubberized coating to prevent shedding and skidding.
- *Sponge rubber* cushions come in either flat (recommended for hard-use areas) or waffled finishes (softer but not as durable). They provide a soft, bouncy feeling underfoot and work best for wall-to-wall installations.
- *Foam rubber*, a medium-weight cushion, also comes in flat and waffled finishes. It's more moderately priced than other types of padding, but still gives good wear for the money.
- *Urethane foam* padding may be one of three types: prime, densified prime, and bonded. Prime offers soft resiliency; densified prime feels extra plush; bonded is the firmest of the three. If you're concerned with floor-level heat or dampness, urethane will be your best cushion choice.

Most cushions are priced according to their weight per square yard. For most areas of the home 40-ounce padding usually is adequate, but for stairs or heavy-traffic areas, a 48-ounce or heavier cushion will perform better.

To test whether the cushion feels firm, yet not so thick that it will cause vacuuming or walking problems, place a sample of the carpet and pad on the floor and walk over it. You can tell quickly whether or not the combination gives you both comfort and resiliency.

Cost and quality
Once you've considered your needs and preferences, you're ready to choose a carpet. Carpet is available in specialty floor covering, department, or home-furnishings stores. It's important to buy from an established retailer who knows his stock and stands behind the quality of his merchandise.

Read carpet labels carefully. A number of manufacturers include such useful information as care and cleaning instructions, decorating advice, and details about fiber content and where the carpet was manufactured. Special labels from fiber producers or suppliers of special treatments also may be included. Retail stores often offer other helpful information about care and cleaning.

Carpet is available in all price ranges from a few dollars per square yard on up. Carpet in upper price ranges generally will be denser, better constructed, and available in a wider choice of colors and styles. If cost is a major factor, compromise on the size or amount of carpet rather than quality, or choose lesser qualities for low-traffic areas.

Find out what price-per-square-yard figures include. Padding and installation may or may not be extra. Remember that you pay the same installation fee regardless of the quality of the carpet, which is another good reason to choose the best material you can afford. Ask who will install the carpet and whether the work is guaranteed; also make sure that you understand delivery and installation dates. Pages 108 and 109 explain how carpet is installed.

If guarantees or warranties are offered, find out who stands behind them—the carpet manufacturer, the fiber producer, or the retailer—and what the terms of the guarantee really mean. Save invoices, labels, and a scrap of carpet for your records.

COMPARING CARPET FIBERS

TYPE	CHARACTERISTICS	ADVANTAGES	DISADVANTAGES	CLEANABILITY
WOOL	Deep, warm, rich look. Very resilient; resists abrasions. Natural, warm feel. Because of cost, used primarily in higher-priced carpets and in custom rugs and carpets.	Excellent durability. Flame resistant. Springy and crush-resistant.	Does not reproduce light or bright shades well. Can be damaged by alkaline detergents. Needs mothproofing.	Greatly resists soil, but cannot be cleaned as easily as synthetic fibers.
ACRYLIC	Closest of synthetic fibers to wool. Non-allergenic; resistant to mildew, moths, and insects. Wide choice of colors available.	Crush resistant and springy. Resists sun fading. Low static generation.	May pill (form bead-like balls of fiber on the face of the carpet).	Cleans very easily. Greatly resists soil because dirt has less tendency to cling to smooth fibers.
MODACRYLIC	Almost always blended with acrylics for carpet.	Abrasion-, mildew-, moth-resistant; non-allergenic. Easily dyed. Is added to acrylic to aid flame resistance.	May tend to pill.	When used in blends, it's easy to clean and maintain.
NYLON	Wide choice of colors and excellent color retention. New nylons have excellent bulk, and are soft to the touch. Special additives make them static free. Good resiliency.	Exceptional durability; strongest man-made fiber. Resists abrasion, mildew, and moths. Continuous-filament fibers minimize pilling, fuzzing, and shedding. Nonallergenic.	Without special additives, nylon can present static-electricity problem. Cut-loop piles will pill.	Can be very resistant to soil stains, most acids, and solvents. Excellent cleanability, even spot cleaning of stains. Hides dirt, so requires less-frequent cleaning.
POLYESTER	Resembles wool in look and touch, and comes in a variety of textures. Good color selection and retention. Resists moths, mildew; is nonallergenic.	Great durability. Almost no pilling or shedding, good abrasion resistance and resiliency. Sheds moisture. Can be used almost anywhere indoors.	Cool to the touch; lacks the "warmth" of other fibers. Is susceptible to oil-based stains.	Good cleanability. Resists most soiling. Has less static electricity buildup than untreated nylon does, so soil clings less.
OLEFIN (POLYPRO-PYLENE)	Primarily styled in loop and random-sheared textures. Is very strong and long wearing, moisture resistant, non-absorbent. Resists abrasion, pilling, and shedding.	Extremely durable. Good for heavy-traffic areas both indoors and out, with proper backing. Fibers can withstand weather and moisture.	In lower grades, may crush and flatten.	Excellent in ease of cleaning. Less static than other fibers, so dirt does not cling. Is the most stain resistant of all present fibers. Resists most acids and chemicals.

AREA RUGS

Although today's area rugs don't fly like Aladdin's, they do perform their own kind of magic—decoratively, that is. To help you decide on one that will be at home in your house, pinpoint the size, price range, and type of rug you want before you begin shopping.

Start by estimating the size rug you need. You can do this by marking out perimeters with string taped to the floor. Most area rugs adhere somewhat to standard sizes (4x6, 6x9, 9x12, 10x14, 12x14), so mark out these measurements first. If none of the regular sizes seems right, consider using two smaller rugs together. Or, you can have many types of rugs custom-made to fit specific spaces.

Set a realistic budget. Depending on the type, size, and quality of a rug, it can cost as little as $50 or more than $5,000. In some cases, an inexpensive rag rug may be more appealing than a costly Oriental. In others, a custom-made dhurrie may be worth its hefty price tag.

As the photo *at left* illustrates, the variety of area rugs is almost overwhelming. Here, and on the following pages, you'll find details about specific types.

Carved rugs

These beautifully patterned rugs combine the underfoot comfort of dense carpet with the decorative versatility of an area rug. Constructed of broadloom carpet, these rugs are inscribed with a carved pattern achieved by selectively trimming areas of the pile. Contrasting borders, fringe, and binding add the finishing touches. A wide variety of predesigned motifs are available, or you can opt to have a custom pattern made just for your room. Color and texture choices are almost limitless. Look for rugs that have thick, dense pile and well-defined carving.

(continued)

AREA RUGS
(continued)

As beautiful as carved rugs are, they are by no means the end of the line in area rugs. In fact, you have so many different types to choose from, you're sure to find one that fits the mood of your home exactly.

Rag, braided, hooked, and woven rugs

The woven, braided, and hooked rugs made in Early America from saved scraps of fabric, yarn, and worn-out quilts are highly treasured for their primitive charm and careful craftsmanship. Today's new rugs—produced using much the same methods—carry on the tradition. Colors range from bright primaries to earth tones and pastels; patterns include stripes, plaids, florals, and folk motifs such as animals and houses. These rugs fit perfectly in today's popular country settings, but they blend with other styles of furnishings as well.

Rugs custom-made for your setting are the most expensive, but they also offer you the widest choices. You can choose size, pattern, and shape, as well as color. Some craftspeople will even dye fabric strips to order in shades to exactly coordinate with your furnishings.

If you're budget-minded, choose a machine-made country-style rug available in department stores and catalogs, or consider hooking or braiding your own rug. Craft books and kits will help you if you take this route. Many patterns are reproductions or adaptations of authentic old designs.

Native American weaving

Colonists and pioneers were not the only early American rug makers. Some of today's most sought-after collectibles are flat-woven Native American rugs, especially those made by the Navaho. The Navaho, a nomadic people, learned weaving from the agrarian Pueblos who raised cotton and produced fine textiles from it. Navaho weavers, however, used only wool, which was introduced to the region by the Spanish conquistadores at the end of the 1500s. The earliest weavings featured stripes, but the Navaho later developed distinctive patterns using diamonds, chevrons, and zigzags. Today, the Navaho produce hand-woven rugs in bright primary colors and in natural shades of black, gray, and tan.

One of the best places to find (and learn about) antique American Indian weavings and other artwork is at an annual show and sale held every summer in Santa Fe, New Mexico. This show is the largest and most prestigious marketplace of its kind in the United States.

Natural-fiber rugs

Primarily imported from India and China, natural-fiber rugs are woven of a variety of grasses and straws. Although most of these inexpensive rugs range from light tan to dark brown, some of the newest designs come in solid primary colors or in pastel-hued patterns. You'll find many different shapes and sizes available; some small squares can join to form a room-size carpet. Although natural-fiber rugs aren't as durable as other types of rugs, they do stand up to normal traffic and demand little care.

A RUG SAMPLER

The outline drawing *above* identifies the area rugs pictured on pages 88 and 89, moving clockwise from upper left.
1. Contemporary sculptured pile rug
2. Machine-made reproduction Bijar Oriental
3. Woven Axminster with bilevel cut pile
4. Braided oval
5. Rich cut pile carved in traditional motifs
6. Multistriped earth-tone dhurrie
7. Pastel-tone dhurrie
8. Woven wool needlepoint
9. Multicolored rag rug
10. Loosely woven dhurrie

Shag rugs

If you prefer a deep, shaggy pile, consider *flokatis* from Greece and *ryas* from Scandinavia. Flokatis are woven by hand from wool yarn that's hand-twisted to give it a fluffy texture. During the weaving process, strands are left loose to create a pile several inches long. The rugs are then placed under local waterfalls, where the water further softens the wool fibers. Flokatis come in white, off-white, gray, and, less frequently, solid bright colors.

Ryas feature a rough, shaggy wool pile and a weave that combines fringes of knotted pile with tapestry weave. Instead of seeing only the top ends of the yarn pile, you see the sides of the strands on the surface. Early ryas were woven as bedspreads in dark colors to hide dirt. Today's ryas come in a multitude of bright colors and usually feature bold abstract geometric patterns.

The countries of the Far and Near East contribute a variety of formal and casual area rugs. The information on the facing page will help you select Orientals, kilims, and dhurries.

ORIENTALS, KILIMS, AND DHURRIES

Antique Orientals are the aristocrats of area rugs, and some command prices in the tens of thousands of dollars. What makes these rugs so expensive? Relative rarity and hand craftsmanship. An Oriental is a one-of-a-kind work of art that took years to create and can last more than a century. Buying one of these rugs certainly is an investment, and a good one at that.

Orientals are by definition handmade, either knotted or flat-woven. Those with a pile are knotted. In this construction the weaver starts by attaching vertical *warp* threads (often made of cotton) to the top and bottom of a loom. Using strands of wool, the weaver then wraps pairs of warp threads together with a knot. The loose ends of these knots form the carpet pile. Horizontal *weft* threads are then woven across the rug to secure the knots. The color and placement of the knots form the carpet pattern, like colored squares on a graph-paper grid. The finest Orientals can have several hundred knots per square inch. High knot counts let the weaver create intricate curved designs; fewer knots result in a coarser rug with more angular geometric patterns.

Recognizing the genuine article

Understanding how an Oriental is made lets you tell the difference between an authentic Oriental rug and a machine-made rug with an Oriental design.

Separate the pile and look at the base of the fibers. If the rug is machine-made, you won't see the knots characteristic of hand workmanship. Next, turn the rug over. In a handmade rug the loops of the knots will be clearly visible on

the back, falling into the same well-defined pattern as the front. In contrast, the pattern on the back of a machine-made rug is indistinct, and you'll often notice continuous straight lines running the length of the rug.

Finally, examine the fringe. In a genuine Oriental, it's an extension of the warp threads. In machine-made rugs, the fringe is sewn on and is not an integral part of the rug's body.

Color and design

Traditional Orientals have been woven in Iran (formerly Persia), Turkey, Turkestan, China, India, Pakistan, and the Caucasus regions of the Soviet Union. Within each broad area, cities and regions (such as Kashan, Shiraz, and Kazbek) produced rugs with distinctive local patterns. At one time design and area of origin were one and the same, but today you might find a traditional Kashan pattern, for example, reproduced by an Indian weaver.

Colors range from the rich reds of Persian rugs to the clear pastel shades favored by the Chinese. Most Oriental rugs are rectangular with a central field, or ground, surrounded by patterned borders. The fields vary widely from region to region but fall into four basic categories.
● *Medallion* designs feature a central medallion or several medallions. The background may be open (a solid color), filled with a small overall pattern, or semi-open (scattered with small motifs).
● *Repeat* designs consist of rows of the same motif. Often the motifs are diamond-shaped medallions called *guls*.
● An *allover* design has little repetition and often features one large scene such as a hunt, garden, or tree of life.

● *Prayer rugs* are easily recognized by a distinctive arch in the pattern. Called a *mihrab,* it represents the niche in a Moslem mosque that faces Mecca.

If you're considering purchasing an Oriental, consult some of the many books on the subject to familiarize yourself with typical patterns and color combinations.

Where to buy an Oriental

Your best source for genuine Orientals is a reputable, established dealer. This dealer will have a wide selection to choose from, and a reputation to maintain. Take your time, and visit several dealers before making your selection. Most dealers will let you take a rug home for a trial period, and you should take advantage of this practice. You'll be able to see how the rug looks in the setting you've planned for it, and have plenty of time to examine its quality.

Be wary of traveling auctioneers selling out of hotel or motel rooms. You'll rarely get a bargain, as the rugs will not be sold for less than a predetermined price that ensures a profit for both the auctioneer and the consignor. In addition, the auctioneer sometimes has some confederates in the audience whose job is to bid up the price. If you do purchase a rug, you'll have a hard time returning or exchanging it if you're dissatisfied with it.

Less-expensive alternatives

If a hand-knotted Oriental is out of your price range, you may want to choose a machine-made Oriental-style rug. Many are of excellent quality and often come in a wider range of colors than do handmades, although they won't appreciate in value the

way a genuine Oriental will. Reproductions with woven patterns are far superior to those made by printing a design onto a plain carpet.

For a different look and texture, consider a *kilim*. A kilim is a flat-woven, pileless wool rug that looks like a tapestry. The pattern is made by weaving different colored wefts in and out of the warp threads. It takes much less time to weave a kilim than to knot a pile rug, making the kilims generally less costly. Kilims are sometimes referred to as "tribal rugs" after the nomadic weavers who make them. They commonly feature bright colors and geometric patterns or stripes, and are usually less formal in mood than knotted Orientals.

When you inspect a kilim, you can't count knots per square inch. To determine the fineness of the weave, count the number of vertical warp threads and horizontal wefts in a given section.

A variant of the kilim is the Indian *dhurrie,* a flat-woven rug traditionally made of cotton. Once considered the poor cousin of Oriental carpets, dhurries are now looked upon as decorating assets in their own right. Traditional dhurries were woven in bright colors and featured stripes or cultural motifs. Indian rug makers are now modifying their designs to reflect the tastes of the western market. You can now find dhurries made of wool as well as cotton. Many feature muted pastel tones and abstract patterns or modern adaptations of classic geometric patterns. You also can have dhurries custom-woven in your choice of colors and pattern. Like kilims, dhurries are reversible which doubles their lifetime.

RESILIENT FLOORING

Examine the photo here and you'll see that resilient flooring has come of age. Today's technology makes it possible to create long-lasting products that look like almost any material imaginable. The multiple appeals of durability, easy maintenance, and up-to-date colors, patterns, and textures make resilient flooring an especially good choice for hard-use rooms such as kitchens, baths, and family rooms.

Resilient flooring falls into two broad categories: sheet goods, which are sold in rolls, and tiles. Most sheet goods and many tiles are made of vinyl, which is either solid or blended with other materials. In addition to vinyl tiles, you can find rubber, asphalt, and cork tiles, although the last two materials are hard to obtain today.

Sheet flooring

Resilient sheet flooring comes in 6-, 9-, and 12-foot widths, which make it possible to avoid seams in all but very large rooms. Although sheet flooring is more expensive than comparable grades of vinyl tiles, it offers more colors and patterns.

Sheet vinyl can go on almost any floor, including below-ground-level or "below-grade" basements. The few exceptions are products with backings made of cellulose felt that don't stand up to damp conditions. Ask your dealer about below-grade applications before you make a selection.

In areas where surface moisture levels are high, such as kitchens, baths, and laundry rooms, sheet goods are recommended over tiles.

Over a long period of time, moisture could seep down through the floor's seams and loosen the tiles' adhesive.

Today, two kinds of sheet flooring are made: *inlaid* and *rotovinyl*. Inlaid vinyls are made of solid vinyl and are considered "top of the line." Their surface is built up, layer by layer, of tiny vinyl or polyurethane granules fused under heat and pressure. Inherently thick and soft, some inlaid vinyls have extra layers of foam to provide added comfort underfoot and to muffle noise.

Although inlaid vinyls cost considerably more than other types, they last longer. The colors and patterns don't wear off because they go all the way through the material to the backing.

Inlaids are heavier than other resilient floorings, so they're more difficult to install. In cases where inlaids are permanently installed in the home, it's best to have the job done by a professional who can make sure the seams are tight and the patterns match. However, if sheet goods are to be cut and fitted for a loose-lay application—simply stapled around the edges rather than cemented to the floor—you can probably handle the task yourself, as explained on pages 112 and 113.

Rotovinyl floor coverings are produced in a process that combines photography with printing. The photography allows realistic simulation of materials such as stone, brick, slate, and wood.

(continued)

RESILIENT FLOORING
(continued)

RESILIENT FLOORING OPTIONS

TYPE	CHARACTERISTICS	USES	ADVANTAGES
VINYL COMPOSITION TILE 	Available in solid colors, marbleized patterns, and textured finishes. Resists alkalis, easily installed, low cost.	Above, on, and below grade; on concrete, wood floors, and metal, plywood, or hardboard subfloors; over radiant heating.	Excellent durability; resistant to grease, moisture, acids, burns, denting, and chipping.
SOLID VINYL TILE 	Often simulates natural materials. Also comes in clear solid colors.	Above, on, and below grade.	Easy to install; excellent durability; resists grease, moisture, alkalis, acids, denting, and chipping.
RUBBER TILE 	Handsome, clear colors in a limited range of textures.	Above, on, and below grade (be sure to check with manufacturer because some tiles have restricted use); on-grade concrete.	Excellent resilience, quiet, durable.
SHEET VINYL 	Wide range of colors, patterns, and surface finishes. Inlaid types have vinyl all the way through; rotovinyls feature a photographic image just below a clear vinyl surface.	Above, on, and below grade.	Good resilience and durability; extra comfort underfoot if cushioned.

DISADVANTAGES	CLEANABILITY
Not quiet or very resilient.	Easily cleaned with a damp mop.
Fair resilience; burns can mar.	Easily maintained; resists stains.
Expensive; slippery when wet if not textured; some not greaseproof.	Resists dents and stains, but hurt by strong detergents and grease. Buff to maintain glossy surface.
More expensive than comparable grades of tile; often requires professional installation, especially for inlaid vinyls.	Easily maintained, some with no-wax finish.

Once the photographic image is printed, a wear layer of clear vinyl or polyurethane goes on top. The layer's thickness determines how long the rotovinyl floor will look good. For reasonable quality, you need at least 10 mils of topcoat. The most expensive rotovinyls have wear layers 25 mils thick.

Check the amount of cushioning on the back of rotovinyl flooring by squeezing or stepping on a sample. It should be soft but firm. Next, dig a thumbnail into the cushion; the indentation should quickly recover.

Rotovinyls are easier to handle and install than inlaid types. Many products come with their own installation kits. Others need no adhesives. (See pages 110-113 for detailed information about installing resilient flooring materials.)

Resilient tiles

Resilient tiles, which are available in 9- and 12-inch squares, are easy for a do-it-yourselfer to install. Most are self-stick, so you can lay a floor in an afternoon. They also provide decorative flexibility. With a little imagination, you can use different colored and patterned tiles to create your own one-of-a-kind floor.

The two most popular types of tiles are *solid vinyl* and *vinyl composition*. Like solid vinyl sheet goods, solid vinyl tiles are top-of-the-line materials. The tiles' wear layer goes all the way through to the back so they last longer. Solid vinyl tiles come in a wide variety of patterns and colors and are easy on the feet.

Vinyl composition tiles, also called "vct" in the industry, combine vinyl resins with filler materials. They're moderately priced yet long wearing and resistant to burns. Vinyl composition tiles also resist dents, scuffing, and grease.

Other types of floor tiles include asphalt, cork, and rubber. Asphalt tiles were the first kind of resilient tile made. They're inexpensive and can be installed both above and below grade, but are not widely available anymore. Because asphalt tiles are brittle, and stain and dent easily, vinyl composition tiles have taken their place.

Cork tiles also may be difficult to find, since the raw products needed to make cork are growing scarce. Unless coated with vinyl, they're susceptible to staining. Cork tiles are attractive and very resilient, however, and provide good wear in light-traffic areas.

Rubber tiles are manufactured primarily for commercial installations, but are at home in a house, too—and with handsome results. Ribbed or studded rubber tiles, such as those pictured on the preceding page, provide good traction underfoot and work well in high-tech settings. They are costly, however, and some are not recommended for use below grade.

The chart *at left* will help you evaluate resilient flooring materials and choose the ones that will work best for you.

No-wax surfaces

Resilient sheet goods and tiles that are labeled "no-wax" have specially formulated finishes that require minimum maintenance, resist scuffing and staining, and need no waxing. In fact, wax would only dull the finish and shouldn't be used. In time, however, areas of heavy use may dull slightly. To restore these spots to a higher gloss, ask your dealer for a special vinyl dressing.

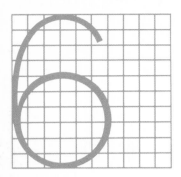

CHOOSING AND BUYING OTHER FLOORING MATERIALS

Some of the best-looking and most stylish floors are made of nonresilient or hard-surface materials such as wood, tile, slate, marble, and brick. You may need professional help to install some of these materials, and a few call for more specialized maintenance than do other kinds of floors. But, carefully chosen and properly cared for, all stand up beautifully to the wear and tear of everyday life, and look great doing it.

SLATE, MARBLE, AND BRICK

Slate, marble, and brick have always been outdoor attractions, forming the solid base for countless patios and pavements. However, they grace a wide variety of indoor living areas, as well. Although nonresilient materials are hard underfoot, their good looks help them fit into virtually all rooms.

Slate
An extremely dense, fine-grained stone, slate possesses notable durability. It won't absorb water (which makes it a little slippery when wet), fights off stains exceptionally well, and is fairly simple to clean.

Though slate is characteristically gray, you'll also find it in other colors. The most common finish, called "natural cleft," is mildly rough to the touch and has some variation in texture. Smoother sand-rubbed finishes also are readily available.

Slate usually comes in 6-inch-square, ½-inch-thick tiles, but larger rectangular shapes, some measuring as much as 18x24 inches, are also frequently used. Most tiles are installed by laying them in a bed of portland cement, a job skilled amateurs can handle on their own.

Brick
Paving bricks, or pavers, are among the least expensive and most eye-appealing materials you can buy. They're rugged, easy to maintain, and come in colors ranging from standard earth tones to more exotic pinks and reds.

Although bricks come in many shapes and sizes, they share one feature: All are made of moist clay and hardened by heat into durable building or paving materials.

You'll discover not only the customary rectangles, but also squares and hexagons, in thicknesses from ¼ to 2½ inches.

Laying bricks without mortar is well within the range of most do-it-yourselfers. For interior surfaces, however, most people lean to the more finished look that mortared joints can provide. Installing a mortared brick floor is a job for a professional.

Marble
Not as overpoweringly expensive as it once was, marble is still a costly flooring material. Even so, its cool, luxurious elegance makes it an excellent choice for master bathrooms and dining rooms. For the budget-minded, it can add an impressive touch of luxury to small but important areas of the house, such as entrances or hallways.

Marble has some definite disadvantages besides its high price (see page 99), but in terms of appearance and variety it has few if any rivals. Marble slabs, in sizes up to 40 square feet, come in a virtually unlimited number of colors. Marble tiles, ½ inch thick and between 8 and 12 inches square, are available in fewer tones, but the selection is still varied.

Commonly used types include calcite, dolomite, serpentine, onyx, and travertine. All have their own characteristic shadings and markings. For example, onyx usually has straight, parallel bands of alternating colors.

(continued)

brick

marble

slate

SLATE, MARBLE,
AND BRICK
(continued)

COMPARING SLATE, MARBLE, AND BRICK

MATERIAL	EFFECT
 **SLATE**	In addition to geometric shapes, slate also comes in irregular pieces. Though dark gray is the most common color, you'll also find stone that's black, blue, blue-black, green, purple, mottled green-purple, and red. Some slate has a solid color throughout *(clear stock);* other material shows off bands of darker shades *(ribbon stock).* Design possibilities are varied. For example, you can create an interesting visual effect by contrasting slate with different grains and textures or by fashioning a multitone floor using slate of complementary hues.
 **MARBLE**	The true aristocrat of all flooring materials, marble provides a smooth, glamorous, almost opulent surface. It comes in a rainbow of colors: for marble slabs—black-gray, blue-gray, brown-yellow, green, pink, white, white-blue, white-brown, black, grayish pink, yellow, and more; for tiles—black, gray, brown, rose, white, and blue. Most marbles used in residential flooring have either a polished *(gloss)* or satin *(honed)* finish.
 **BRICK**	For the homeowner with an artistic nature, brick may be just the thing. If you're so inclined, the different sizes, shapes, and colors provide the freedom to create a unique floor. For example, you can combine a number of patterns in one surface or use mortar joints of various thicknesses and colors—or both. Brick also works remarkably well with other hard-surface coverings. In fact, a cost-conscious way to use marble is to employ it as an accent material laid into an otherwise inexpensive brick floor.

DURABILITY	USES	INSTALLATION	COST
Slate has outstanding durability and is highly stain resistant (no sealers necessary). It tends to scuff in heavily traveled areas, however, and requires occasional waxing. From time to time, joints may need to be scoured and treated with a mildew retardant. Otherwise, periodic wet-mopping will keep the floor looking its best.	It tends to get a bit slippery when wet, so using slate in a bathroom is not advisable. Other than that, slate's diverse range of textures and colors makes it an attractive candidate for most of your home's main living areas.	Slate can be laid in a bed of adhesive or without mortar joints at all. Both are simple methods a careful amateur can handle, but they limit the sizes and shapes you're able to use. Most people still prefer the look of slate laid in concrete, which is a job best left to an experienced pro.	Slate is moderately expensive; if it has to be shipped a considerable distance, it can become very expensive because it is heavy. Add material costs for providing a suitable subsurface and labor costs for installing the floor, and the final bill can be quite high, though not as high as for marble.
Of the various nonresilient floor coverings, marble is the hardest to maintain. Although most marbles are acceptably durable, types vary in their ability to withstand wear and abrasion. All stain easily. Regular cleaning, sealing, and polishing are necessary to keep them in tip-top condition.	Because it's so costly and so formal, marble works best when used judiciously: to set the tone in an elegant dining room, for instance, or create a luxurious atmosphere in a hallway. To save money, use it as an accent material with less expensive floorings.	On the proper subfloor, marble tiles can be laid as easily as their resilient counterparts (though cutting marble is much more difficult). Installing larger slabs, however, is something *only* a marble contractor or subcontractor should do.	Large marble slabs are the most expensive hard-surface floor coverings on the market. Thinner tiles are less costly but still relatively high priced compared with other materials. Including installation charges, the total bill is likely to be as impressive as the floor itself.
Although rugged looking and reliably durable, brick needs a little pampering. Apply a penetrating sealer to a new floor, and top it off with two thin coats of buffable wax. Then wax and polish every six months or so. Damp-mop to clean. Avoid using old paving bricks. Though beautiful, they're likely to chip and crack.	Naturally enough, brick is an inspired choice for rooms with a country or rustic flavor. And, like slate, it's the perfect material to use in living areas that flow out to patios featuring a similar hard-surface base.	Nonresilient floors must be laid on an unswervingly smooth, level surface. Brick is no exception. If you're planning a mortarless installation, make sure the subfloor is sunk, unless you're using very thin pavers, so the bricks will be even with adjacent flooring materials. You may need to double up on joists to handle the extra weight of a brick floor.	Few floor coverings do such a good job for so little money. Although prices vary, thin, rectangular bricks are more economical than less conventional shapes and sizes; still, no type of brick is especially costly.

WOOD

unfinished strip

Not too long ago, it seemed everyone was covering wood with vast expanses of wall-to-wall carpeting or resilient floorings. Now, however, wood has re-established itself as one of the warmest, best-looking, and most durable materials around. To many people, it's a cut above other kinds of flooring materials.

Hardwood is the people's choice, with oak (by far the most popular) and maple leading the way. Nevertheless, softwoods—pine is an excellent example—look as good and wear just as well. Manufacturers, using improved techniques, have added different varieties—birch, beech, and pecan, for instance—to the supply of serviceable and attractive materials. In recent years, some wood floors, impregnated with special plastics, have been made even more durable.

In any case, making selections is a buyer's dream: You can choose from a stunning array of styles, colors, and finishes, in a comfortably wide range of prices—whatever you need to further a decorating scheme. (For a description of wood-floor finishes, see pages 120 and 121.) For a more detailed comparison of different types, read the chart on pages 102 and 103.

Distinguishing traits

No matter what the type or price, nearly all wood is roughly equal in strength and durability. Unlike some materials, for which how much you pay is directly related to how soon you will have to purchase replacements, wood at all price levels should be a trustworthy floor covering for years and years.

The expensive options, or grades, do have a major advantage: progressively more eye appeal thanks to nicer graining and fewer imperfections. The highest-quality grade is *clear,* meaning it's free of knots and other surface flaws. Next, in descending order, are *select, No. 1 common, No. 2 common,* and, finally, the least expensive wood, *1½-foot shorts,* which are basically leftovers from the other grades.

When you're in the market, try to visualize the aesthetic role you'd like a wood floor to play. A costly grade may be an elegant solution for a living room or dining room, whereas seemingly imperfect alternatives might be the perfect way to give a family room or playroom an appealingly rustic character and save money at the same time.

You can buy all grades and types either finished or unfinished. Prefinished flooring costs more and requires careful installation to avoid damaging the wood. Laying unfinished flooring requires less surgical precision, but it usually demands at least some light sanding to smooth small surface irregularities. (To learn about finishing wood floors, see pages 120 and 121.)

(continued)

A PRODUCT OF BRUCE HARDWOOD FLOORS
DALLAS, TEXAS 75248, A TRIANGLE PACIFIC COMPANY
THE WORLD'S LARGEST MAKER OF HARDWOOD FLOORING

random plank

prefinished
strip

parquet
block

WOOD

(continued)

COMPARING WOOD FLOORINGS

MATERIAL	EFFECT
 **PARQUET**	Occasionally referred to as block flooring, parquet usually comes in 6- or 9-inch squares made of short strips laid in geometrical patterns—a mosaic done in wood. Oak, teak, and walnut are the most common materials; basket weave and herringbone are the most popular patterns, but other woods and shapes are widely available. You can buy prefinished squares in many different tones or purchase unfinished wood to stain and seal any color or sheen you want, from matte to high gloss.
 **WOOD TILES**	Wood tiles are similar to parquet squares. The biggest difference is that tiles are not mosaic patterns; instead, they feature the natural grains of solid wood. Oak and maple are the most common materials. Available in 6-, 9-, and 12-inch squares, $\frac{5}{16}$ or $\frac{3}{8}$ of an inch thick, tiles come either unfinished or prefinished in a wide range of wood tones (some are intentionally distressed, that is, made to look old, with scratches or other signs of wear or unevenness). Many have a self-adhesive backing, which makes installation easy and inexpensive.
 **WOOD STRIPS**	The most frequently used type of wood flooring, strips are long, narrow boards, typically measuring 2¼ or 2½ inches wide and about ¾ inch thick (although other widths and thicknesses are commonly available). Strips are tongue-and-grooved and end-matched. Oak, with its coarse, open grain and reddish or brownish cast, is the most popular material; medium-brown maple, dark-brown walnut, and rugged teak and pecan are also handsome choices. Strips come either prefinished or unfinished.
 **WOOD PLANKS**	Wood planks are wider than strips, up to 12 inches wide (and sometimes more). The added dimension is a key to their unsurpassed beauty: It shows off the wood to greater effect than narrower strips. Most planks are made of oak or pine, come in random widths (hence the term "random-plank" floor), and are tongue-and-grooved along the edges. Some floors of this type are pegged with wood or brass for extra visual appeal. Prefinished boards are available, as are those that can be glued, rather than nailed, in place.

DURABILITY	USES	INSTALLATION	COST
Like other wood floors, parquet is highly durable, though it doesn't stand up as well to heavy traffic as strip flooring does. For extra protection, apply two thin coats of wax to newly finished floors or unwaxed prefinished squares. Dry-mop or vacuum often.	Because it presents a fairly formal look, parquet flooring works best in living rooms, dining rooms, quiet family rooms, or other traditional settings.	Fairly easy to install, using an adhesive on a smooth, clean, and level plywood base, but remove resilient flooring first. Installation on a concrete slab is more difficult, but still possible for a handy do-it-yourselfer. Some squares have a self-stick backing.	Relatively costly compared with wood tiles; prefinished squares are more expensive than unfinished materials. However, do-it-yourselfers can save on installation charges.
Very durable, like all wood. Maintenance is similar to that for parquet flooring.	Tiles are an excellent choice for any living area in the house, but they're an especially good option for cost-conscious kitchen remodelers who want the warm feeling of wood without the expense of strip or plank flooring.	Like that for parquet squares. Laid over the proper subfloor, prefinished tiles with self-stick backing can be installed and ready to use in a matter of hours.	Just the thing for really tight budgets. The most costly tiles are about the same price as the least expensive oak strips.
All wood strips are superbly strong flooring materials. Some species are slightly more durable than others, but the difference is negligible. As with other types of wood, frequently vacuum or dry-mop. Occasional waxing benefits appearance and durability.	No other type of wood floor is so versatile for the money. You can work strips into nearly any decorating scheme—formal or informal, contemporary or traditional—and use them practically anywhere in the house.	Strip flooring must be laid over a clean, sound, and level surface. However, unlike parquet squares and wood tiles, it can't be cemented directly to concrete. Skilled do-it-yourselfers can handle the installation, but professional help is often well worth the money.	Except for tiles, unfinished oak strips are the least expensive wood. Maple and pecan are moderately costly, and teak commands top dollar. Price of prefinished materials often eats up any savings gained from not doing the sanding and finishing yourself.
Like all wood, plank floors need frequent cleaning and periodic waxing. Without adequate ventilation below—in a crawl space, for example—boards tend to "cup," forming sharp ridges above the floor level. Older floors tend to develop gaps between planks.	Random-plank floors, especially the pegged versions, are reminiscent of the materials used in early American homes. They convey a rustic, informal feeling that goes well with a colonial or antique decorating scheme.	Similar to strip flooring. If you're doing the job yourself, carefully plan layout of boards so you don't have to cut one into narrower strips for the last row. Also, try to place shorter planks in the room's center, where they'll probably be covered by a rug.	More expensive than wood strips made from the same material. Pegged boards are slightly more costly than unpegged planks. Prefinished wood carries the highest price tag.

TILE

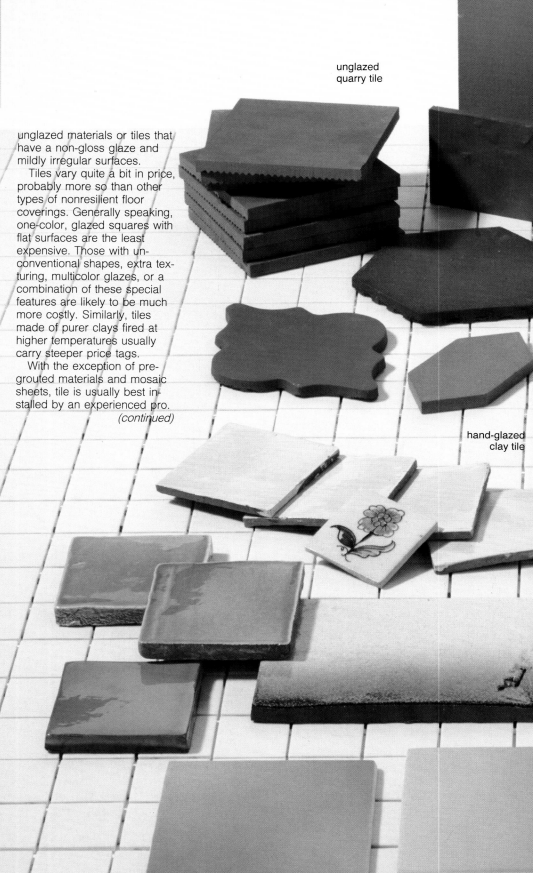

unglazed
quarry tile

hand-glazed
clay tile

Not too long ago, tile was welcomed in many bathrooms, but given the cold shoulder in other living areas. Times have changed, and tile no longer is a one-room wonder.

Few materials can match the beauty, versatility, and durability of a tile floor. Glazed and unglazed ceramic tiles are available in a nearly limitless array of colors, shapes, and sizes. Increasingly popular quarry tile, made of fired, usually unglazed clay, often comes straight from the ground in a warm range of natural earth tones. Smaller mosaic tiles, either glazed or unglazed, are very durable and, because they're mounted together on sheets, are easier for do-it-yourselfers to install.

Further, all tiles are almost everlastingly tough, resist water and stains exceptionally well, and are simpler to maintain than nearly any other hard-surface floor.

The great number of choices, some of which are shown here, prove that tiles aren't just for bathrooms anymore. They make serviceable, eye-catching floors in kitchens, family rooms, dining rooms, utility rooms, halls, entrances—anywhere you want color, interesting pattern and texture, and down-to-earth practicality.

Like other materials, however, tiles do have some disadvantages. They don't possess the springy comfort underfoot that resilients have, and they're distinctly cool to the touch, a chilling fact during the winter but a pleasure during long, hot summers. In addition, most kinds are at least slightly slippery, especially the high-gloss, glazed variety. In bathrooms, therefore, it's wise to stick with

unglazed materials or tiles that have a non-gloss glaze and mildly irregular surfaces.

Tiles vary quite a bit in price, probably more so than other types of nonresilient floor coverings. Generally speaking, one-color, glazed squares with flat surfaces are the least expensive. Those with unconventional shapes, extra texturing, multicolor glazes, or a combination of these special features are likely to be much more costly. Similarly, tiles made of purer clays fired at higher temperatures usually carry steeper price tags.

With the exception of pregrouted materials and mosaic sheets, tile is usually best installed by an experienced pro.

(continued)

ceramic
mosaic

glazed
ceramic

hand-glazed
clay tile

American
Olean
Tile

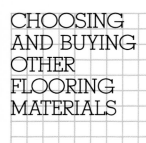
TILE
(continued)

COMPARING TILE FLOORINGS

MATERIAL	EFFECT

GLAZED TILE

The beautiful jewellike glaze fused to clay tile bodies gives them an exquisitely rich look. Sizes range from 2x4-inch rectangles to 1-foot squares, but the most common dimensions are 4¼ inches square and ⁵⁄₁₆ inch thick. You'll find a wide choice of colors, glazes, patterns, and shapes, including octagons, hexagons, triangles, and curves, along with the standard rectangles and squares.

UNGLAZED TILE

Unlike glazed material, in which color is added to the surface of the tile form before final baking, unglazed tile has pigment running through the entire body—either natural earth tones or hues mixed with the clay before the tile is formed and baked. The dull, unassuming finish is often a decorating plus. Sizes and shapes are similar to those of glazed tile.

MOSAIC TILE

Ceramic mosaics are small tiles; most are 1- and 2-inch squares or 1x2-inch rectangles, ¼ inch thick, although typical mosaic shapes also include hexagons and a combination of squares and rectangles. Much mosaic tile is unglazed, with pigment added to the material, coloring it throughout. Also available are glazed mosaic patterns in a variety of different shapes and sizes up to 3 inches across.

QUARRY TILE

Unglazed, unpatterned quarry tile is made from natural clays in large sizes—6- to 8-inch squares and 4x8-inch rectangles, usually about ½ inch thick. Earth tones—reds, browns, and buffs—dominate the market, but you should be able to find other colors, such as white, yellow, and green, as well. Irregular shapes and decorative textures are also available, and some quarry tiles are glazed.

DURABILITY	USES	INSTALLATION	COST
Easy to care for. Periodic damp-mopping with water and a mild detergent will keep it clean; occasional rubbing with a dry towel will bring back faded luster. From time to time, scrub the grout with a solution of water and household bleach.	Tiles wear well and provide acceptable traction. Use them anywhere—except in bedrooms—but they're especially good in kitchens, baths, and entryways. Avoid using high-gloss (and therefore slippery) materials on floors.	A patient amateur with above-average skills can do the job, using an organic adhesive and tile cutter. However, large areas of tile are best left to a pro, unless you're working with pregrouted sheets. All tile must be laid over a smooth, dead-level surface.	Inexpensive to expensive, depending on glazing, texture, shape, and thickness. Pregrouted sheets are high priced.
Very durable. Unglazed tile is less slippery than glazed and doesn't show wear as soon because color permeates the whole tile. Unglazed tile will, however, stain easily and needs a protective sealer. To clean, damp-mop regularly; scrub grout occasionally.	Effective in nearly any living area, unglazed tile is particularly useful in entryways and rooms that lead out to patios and pavements featuring complementary hard-surface materials.	Like that for glazed material. Because all floor tile resists water and can withstand very cold temperatures, you can lay it below-grade on a basement concrete floor without installing a subsurface.	Inexpensive to expensive, depending on texture, shape, and thickness. As with glazed tile, pregrouted sheets are more costly.
Both glazed and unglazed versions are extremely rugged. Maintenance is similar to that for other kinds of tile—occasional damp-mopping will keep it looking good. Narrow grout joints are sometimes tough to scrub clean.	One of the most common bathroom materials around, mosaic tile also is highly effective as a floor covering in kitchens and entryways.	A do-it-yourselfer's delight. Mounted on 1x1- or 1x2-foot sheets that are either faced with paper or backed by non-removable mesh, mosaics can be laid in a bed of adhesive much faster, and with fewer problems, than individual tiles.	More costly than the least expensive glazed and unglazed tiles, mosaics are nevertheless a real bargain if you install them yourself.
Because of its extra thickness, the most durable of all floor tiles. Like other unglazed materials, unglazed quarry tile should have a sealer coat to ward off stains. Clean and maintain as you would similar surfaces.	Ideal for heavily traveled areas—kitchens and entryways, to name two. Earth tones make them a natural for rustic or country decorating schemes.	Fairly difficult. You might try laying small floors yourself, but leave larger surfaces to a pro.	Moderately expensive, though not nearly so high as tiles with special textures, patterns, and glazes. Installation costs will boost the final bill.

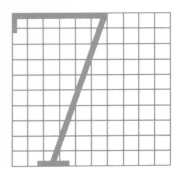

INSTALLING NEW FLOORING MATERIALS

Putting a new floor or floor covering in even one room of your home can be a major expense, and installation is no small part of the total. Some types of flooring—resilient tiles, for example—lend themselves to do-it-yourself efforts; others—such as wall-to-wall carpeting—often are best left to professionals. Before you make any purchasing decisions, read up on the details of installation techniques. Whether you choose to do the work yourself or hire someone else to do it, knowing how it should be done will help ensure an installation of lasting quality.

CARPET

If you have ever watched a professional carpet installer at work, you know that putting down wall-to-wall carpet is back-straining, knee-jarring labor. Handling the heavy materials and stretching them into position are no easy jobs; the extra cost of professional carpet installation generally is included in the quoted price per yard, and it's usually well worth it.

Nevertheless, it's a good idea to know how carpet should be laid. Then you'll have a standard by which to judge the work done at your house, and a starting point in case you decide to install new carpet on your own.

From the bottom up
Wall-to-wall carpeting can go over almost any type of flooring, from vinyl to hardwood to concrete. The flooring must be level and in good condition, however. If it is uneven, plane down high spots and use floor-leveling compound to fill dips. If the floor is in very poor condition, consider installing a new underlayment of ¼-inch or thicker plywood or waferboard. Also, if you plan to lay the carpet in a below-grade area, such as a basement, make sure no surface moisture gets trapped below the new covering.

Prepare for the installation by removing all furniture and obstacles from the room. Also carefully remove baseboard shoe moldings. You'll put them back when the installation is done.

If you are installing the carpet yourself, unroll it completely before you begin to cut it. Inspect it for defects and to make sure you have received the amount you ordered.

First steps
Tackless strips, which create a framework that the carpet will be stretched over and secured to, must be installed around the perimeter of the room. Where two carpeted room areas join, the strips are unnecessary; the two carpets will be seamed together later. Where carpeting adjoins a non-carpeted floor, metal thresholds often are installed to cover the carpet edges and keep them from fraying.

The next step—unless you have purchased integral-pad carpet, which has its own fused backing—is to install the pad. The shiny side should face up, and the pad should be cut to fit within the strip framework. Staple the pad to wood or resilient floors; use pad adhesive on concrete. Be sure seam lines and edges are well secured.

Cutting corners
Now it's time to cut the carpet to room dimensions, allowing some excess for trimming later. Once the carpet is sized, a knee kicker helps smooth, tighten, and secure the edges. Then, after an edge is secured, a power stretcher pulls the carpet to the opposite wall. Finally, all edges are trimmed with a special carpet-trimming tool or a utility knife.

Seams are joined with a special heat-setting tape that bonds to the carpet backing as the carpet is pressed down over it. After the edges are trimmed, they are folded back; then the tape is laid on the floor along the seam line and a special heating iron run along the tape to melt it.

1 The first step in carpet installation is to lay a framework of tackless strips around the room's perimeter. The strips should be nailed or stapled about ⅜ to ½ inch away from the wall, to allow for tucking. The pins on the strips must face the wall.

2 The carpet is measured and rough-cut, allowing ample excess. Carpet with a loop pile should be cut from the front, carpet with cut pile from the back. Slits should be made in the carpet face to accommodate obstructions such as door jambs.

3 The next step is to secure the carpet to one wall, using a knee kicker to force the carpet backing securely onto the tackless strips. Then a power stretcher helps bring the rest of the goods into place.

4 Trimming, using a utility knife or a carpet trimmer, is the final task. After the trimming, ¼ inch will remain to be tucked between the tackless strip and the wall or baseboard. A wide-blade masonry knife is good for tucking.

INSTALLATION POINTERS: RESILIENT TILE

1 Determine the midpoint of each wall of the room. Drive a nail into the floor below each midpoint. Stretch a chalked string between the opposite walls and snap it against the floor. Use a carpenter's square to check the angle where the lines intersect.

2 Remove any base moldings before you start laying the tile. Using a saw, cut away a fraction of an inch of the bottoms of door jambs or casings to allow space for the resilient tile to slide into place beneath them.

4 Measure carefully when fitting tiles around door frames. Transfer the dimensions to a tile, then cut the desired shape with a utility knife or shears. You may need to use a paper pattern for cutting around pipes or other intricate shapes.

5 Check the cut by sliding the tile into position before removing the paper backing or spreading the mastic. Recut to adjust if necessary, and then install the tile. Heating the tile can make it easier to cut.

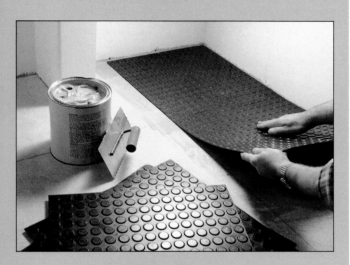

3 If you are using mastic, spread it thinly over one section of floor at a time. Lay the first tile where the base lines intersect; square subsequent tiles with the lines. With rubber tiles, you can start at a corner of the room, because seams aren't noticeable.

6 After all tiles have been laid, ensure a tight bond by rolling the floor in both directions with a 150-pound roller. You can rent rollers from flooring contractors, or use an ordinary household rolling pin instead and bear down on it with your full weight.

Resilient floor tiles have been popular with do-it-yourselfers for decades, although many homeowners also choose to have them professionally installed. Vinyl and vinyl-composition tiles are the most common and the least difficult to work with. Rubber tiles, such as those shown in the box *at left,* are trickier to work with but not beyond the abilities of a proficient handyperson.

If you plan to install any type of resilient tiles yourself, follow the manufacturer's instructions to the letter; seemingly minor variations in technique may be significant because of differences in composition and surface treatment. Certain general procedures are fairly standard, however.

Sound footing
Resilient flooring can be laid over almost any surface except other resilient flooring (some of the newest vinyls, however, are specially treated to go directly over old resilients). Be sure the existing floor, whatever it's made of, is in good condition. Resilient tile will reveal any underlying unevenness or flaws. You may need to install an underlayment of ¼-inch or thicker plywood or hardboard.

If the old floor is in reasonably good condition, clean it throughly and fill any cracks or gaps with a patching compound; if the floor is wood, repair any loose or uneven areas. If you are installing the new floor in a basement room, be sure the tile you have selected is suitable for below-grade installation.

Planning and patterns
Self-stick vinyl or vinyl-composition tiles are the easiest resilients to work with. You just peel off the paper backing, lay the tile carefully in place, kneel on it to make sure it adheres to the subfloor, and go on to the next tile.

If you are using tiles that have no adhesive backing, you will need to purchase adhesive and, unless the adhesive is the brush-on kind, a trowel for spreading it. Use only the type of adhesive recommended by the manufacturer.

Before you start to lay the tiles permanently, do a dry run to be certain that the borders will be even on all sides. Start by determining the midpoints of opposite walls. Snap a chalk line between them and repeat on the other two walls. Check the right angles formed by the two lines to be sure they are perfectly square. Dry-lay the tiles in quadrants, starting where the lines intersect. Adjust for proper border spacing.

Now you can begin the actual installation. Again work one quadrant at a time. Spread the mastic, if required, then lay the first tile square, aligning along the chalk line. Don't slide the tiles into place; instead, butt the edges together, then lay each tile firmly in place.

Cutting and trimming
Use a utility or linoleum knife to cut tiles to size at corners and edges. Warming the tile in an oven or over a lamp will make cutting easier.

To size border tiles, place a loose tile directly over the last full tile closest to the wall. Then put another loose tile on top of this one, but slide it over until it butts against the wall. Use the edge of the top tile as a guide to mark the tile beneath it, and cut along the line.

INSTALLATION POINTERS: SHEET GOODS

1 To create a template for cutting sheet goods to size, use heavy paper or building felt. Join pieces with tape until you have a piece a little larger than the room you will cover. Mark all room and detail measurements on the paper.

2 Fit the template onto the floor, aligning all corners and edges. Using a sharp utility knife, cut the template to the room's exact dimen- sions. Use a compass to scribe cutouts for irregular- ities in the room's outline.

4 If you're not loose-laying sheet goods, be sure to use only the adhesive rec- ommended by the flooring manufacturer. Using a trowel, evenly spread the adhesive across the entire floor; comb out the adhesive with the notched edge of the trowel, as shown.

5 Unroll the sheet, starting at one wall. Be sure that all corners and edges are perfectly aligned. You may need to make final ad- justments around doorways and other irregularities as you work. Use a compass for scribing.

3 Once the template pattern is perfect, lay it on top of the unrolled sheet goods, with right sides of both up. Trace the pattern on the flooring material with a pencil. Then cut out the design, using a linoleum knife with a straightedge as a guide.

6 Once the sheet is laid, use a small hand roller, like the ones used for hanging wallpaper, to help bond the edges. Install base molding as a finishing touch. Molding also helps to secure edges around the perimeter of the room.

Most resilient sheet flooring, like most carpeting, is installed by professionals, and with good reason. Sheet material, which comes in widths of 6, 9, 12, and 15 feet, is heavy and hard to handle; any seams must be tight; and because the effect of sheet flooring is intended to be sweeping and all of a piece, patterns must match precisely at the seams.

Some cushioned vinyl sheet flooring, however, is specially designed for loose-lay installation. Although the problems of weight and precise measurement remain, loose-laying sheet flooring is a task handy homeowners can tackle.

As with other types of new flooring, new sheet goods must go over a smooth, clean, sound surface. Most sheet goods can cover wood, concrete, or existing resilient floorings, as long as they're in good condition. Be sure to remove all shoe moldings before beginning installation.

Size and shape
To determine how to cut sheet goods to fit a given room, you must carefully transfer the room's measurements to the sheet. Or, lay out a pattern of the room's shape and trace it onto the sheet so you can cut the sheet to the correct dimensions. One of the main difficulties in laying sheet goods is finding room to roll out the material first so the dimensions or pattern can be transferred. If the weather permits and outside and inside temperatures are about the same, a *clean, smooth* patio or driveway is a good spot for the task.

If you are laying your own sheet flooring, you'll need to make a template of the room's shape. To do this, join the edges of building felt or heavy pattern paper with heavy tape to make one continuous sheet equal to the full length and width of the room. Then make precise cutouts for doorways and other details. If the room has complex angles, make a scaled plan of the room on graph paper before tackling the template itself. When the template is cut to the room's exact dimensions, transfer the pattern to the sheet goods. Trace the pattern on the right side of the sheet, then cut it with a linoleum knife.

Before you cut the flooring, make sure the starting edge of the material is straight and true. If not, snap a chalk line along it, and cut with heavy-duty shears or a linoleum knife.

Finishing touches
If the sheet goods you have selected require adhesive, the next step after cutting the goods to size is to apply the mastic to the floor. Smoothly spread it with a trowel; do this quickly so you can lay the flooring before the adhesive dries.

If you are installing loose-lay sheet goods, roll up a sheet after cutting, with the starting edge on the outside. Put this edge against the starting wall, unroll it, and trim to fit. Any difficult contour cuts around pipes or doors should be scribed and cut after the goods are in place. When installation is completed, you can camouflage slits with seam-sealing fluid.

Secure loose-lay sheet goods around the perimeter by brushing adhesive on the floor, then pressing the sheet in place. Use shoe moldings to achieve a finished appearance; they will also help secure the flooring. At doorways, use metal strips to protect raw edges.

INSTALLATION POINTERS: HARD-SURFACE TILE

1 Nail guide boards along perpendicular chalk lines snapped from the midpoints of opposite walls. Then dry-lay a row of tiles along the boards. Use tile spacers of wood strips or scrap tile to maintain equal distances between each tile.

2 Now look at the edges. You may need to adjust the field of tiles so the borders on all sides of the room will be equal. Snap a new chalk line to indicate where the border should begin. Start laying the tiles along this line.

4 To fit tile around doorways, measure the cut to be made and mark the location on the tile; or make a pattern of the shape and transfer it to the tile. Cut the tile as shown in photo 3, and fit it snugly into position around the doorway.

5 After laying the tile in place with adhesive, mix the grout. As the photo shows, the grout will just about cover the tiles when you first apply it. Use diagonal pressure across the face of the tiles to distribute the grout evenly.

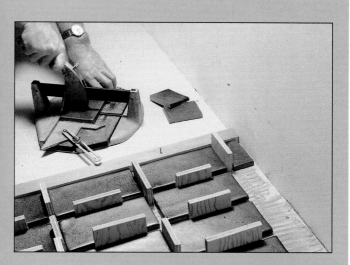

3 To cut the border tiles, mark them as you would resilient tiles (see page 111). Then trim them with a tile cutter, or use a glass cutter and a straightedge. Score the tile on its face; then place it on the edge of a board, face up, and snap it with a downward motion.

6 Use a wet sponge to wash the grout off the face of the tile, then polish with a soft, dry cloth. To prevent grout from mildewing or discoloring, it's a good idea to apply a special-purpose sealer to the grout when it is throughly dry.

Some of the most attractive and desirable flooring available is in the hard-surface family: ceramic, mosaic, and quarry tiles, slate, brick, terrazzo, and marble. Some of these are well suited to do-it-yourself installation; others are not.

Among the least difficult types of hard-surface tile to install is mosaic, which is available in 1- and 2-inch squares mounted on sheets of paper or mesh. Glazed ceramic tiles, pictured in the box *at left,* are also fairly easy to install. They come in sizes from 1-inch to 12-inch squares. Installing materials such as quarry and paving tiles generally calls for highly skilled amateurs, if not professionals.

Special installation concerns

Because hard-surface tiles are rigid and inflexible, they must be mounted on a smooth, solid surface. If the tile is to cover a wood floor, you will need an underlayment of ½-inch exterior-grade cement-surfaced plywood to prevent movement, which could crack the grout between tiles.

Concrete is a good base for tiles, as long as it's perfectly level. Fill low spots with latex or vinyl cement, and sand the surface smooth. Dry-set mortars are good for bonding tiles to concrete.

If you are doing your own tile installation, be sure to use the type of adhesive and grout recommended for the particular tile you are using. Check the flooring manufacturer's instructions, or consult with your tile dealer.

Getting started

Tiles look their best when they are evenly spaced. To ensure that yours will be, you'll need to use spacers when you lay the tile. Make them out of scrap wood or tile before you start to lay the flooring. To figure out the proper layout and spacing, install guide boards and dry-lay the tile as shown *at left.*

Once your layout is plotted, it's time to apply the adhesive. Spread it with the notched edge of a serrated trowel, covering about a 2-foot-square area. The adhesive should form thick ridges, alternating with almost bare valleys. Carefully place each tile into position, turning it slightly to set the adhesive. Then level the tile by tapping it with a board laid across it.

After all the tiles are firmly in place and the adhesive is set, mix the grout according to package instructions. It should have a thick, plasterlike consistency. Use a rubber float or squeegee to apply the grout evenly to the tile. Work it in with diagonal strokes, and make sure ample grout is packed into all joints.

Allow the grout to set for a few minutes. Then, compact the grout by tooling the joints with a rounded object such as a toothbrush handle.

Finally, remove excess grout from the tile surface with a wet sponge. Polish the tiles with a clean, soft cloth.

Special tips for mosaic tiles

Because mosaic tiles are often premounted, they are quicker to lay than individual ceramic tiles. You need to use guide boards and spacers between sheets of tile rather than between individual tiles. Tamp the sheet into the adhesive with a piece of plywood, and wipe away any excess mastic. After the adhesive sets, soak the paper face covering on the sheets with warm water. Peel it off as it loosens. Then grout the tiles.

PARQUET

Parquet blocks, made of wood strips glued together into squares or rectangles, are really tiles made of wood. Consequently, parquet flooring offers the perennial appeal of wood, yet goes down as easily as resilient tile.

Like wood strip flooring (see pages 118 and 119), parquet comes prefinished or unfinished. Prefinished parquet costs more and requires greater care during installation because the surface has to be preserved; unfinished parquet, on the other hand, is easier to install but takes more time because once laid it still has to be sanded and sealed.

Preparation

Parquet flooring can go below grade as well as on or above grade. As with other types of new flooring, it needs a sound base. If your existing flooring is in poor condition, remove it and put down underlayment. If removal is unfeasible, install underlayment over the existing floor.

To lay a parquet floor over concrete, you will first need to put down a layer of poly-ethylene film and install 2x4 sleepers to fur the new floor up off the concrete. Position the sleepers at 16-inch intervals, secure them with adhesive and masonry nails, then nail underlayment to the sleepers.

Special considerations

Because all wood, including parquet, absorbs moisture, it's important to acclimate any new wood flooring to your home before you install it. Do this by spreading the blocks around the room they will be installed in, then let them remain for at least 72 hours. This allows them to adjust to your home's heat and humidity patterns.

Before you start the instal-lation, remove any baseboard shoe moldings, scrape up any paint or plaster on the old floor, countersink all nails, and sweep or vacuum thoroughly. As with resilient tiles, you'll need to undercut the bottoms of all door casings with a handsaw so the parquet blocks will slide in beneath them.

Because a regular pattern is a key factor in the aesthetic success of any parquet floor, it's especially important to create straight and true guide-lines before you lay the blocks. Square off the room with two absolutely perpendicular chalk lines, using a carpenter's square to double-check their intersection. Next, lay a pair of 1x2s along the chalk lines to serve as guide boards for the first quadrant of the room. Now you can start laying the parquet.

The box *opposite* illustrates highlights of the installation of 12-inch-square tongue-and-groove wood blocks. Follow the same general principles to install other types of parquet, as well as resilient tiles.

Installation

If you plan to install your own parquet flooring, you'll find it easiest to work with the adhesive-backed varieties. These have pressure-sensitive glue on their backs, protected until the moment of installation by peel-off paper.

Installing this type of parquet is a matter of lining up rows of wood blocks and placing the tongue of each successive block in the groove of its neighbor. Use a mallet to help tap the blocks firmly into place, striking the back of a second block placed on top of the first to prevent damage to the wood.

Working from the inter-section of the two guide boards, align the bottom edges of the first block and lay it in place. Lay additional blocks along the guide boards, all the way to the wall. When one row is completed, fill in adjacent rows, continuing until the quadrant is filled.

When you have completed the first quadrant, shift your guide boards and start work on the next quadrant.

Problem pieces

Depending on the size of the floor you are covering, laying an adhesive-backed parquet floor may take as little as three hours. The most time-consuming part of the job will be fitting the wood blocks around irregular features in the room, completing borders, and final touches, such as mold-ings, that will give the floor a professionally installed look. Allow at least as much time for details of this kind as for the rest of the task.

When you encounter a wall and must cut a border of blocks to fit, the best technique is to scribe the measurement on a loose block. Lay a block on top of the last one laid near the wall. On top of this block, lay a second loose one, butting it adjacent to the wall. Using the edge of this block as your guide, draw a line on the block beneath it. Before making your cut, be sure to add ½ inch to allow for expansion of the wood. Then make your cuts with either a saber saw or a table saw.

To accommodate odd shapes, such as curves or acute angles, consider using the backing papers of the wood blocks as templates. Slip one of the papers into each hole to be filled. Draw the cutting line on the paper, leaving ½ inch for expansion on the outer edge. Trim the paper and use it as your pattern to transfer the shape to a block. Then cut the parquet to fit.

When you buy parquet tile for do-it-yourself installation, you will probably also find a variety of special moldings for finishing the project, too. Among the most important of these are reducer strips, which bridge the gap between the new parquet and existing flooring in adjacent rooms. You should install a reducer strip at each doorway. Cut notches in the strip as needed to fit around the door stops; then secure the strip with countersunk nails.

Still other special moldings are available. Some that may prove especially useful are stair moldings, ½-inch quarter rounds for the baseboard shoe, and threshold moldings for a transition between parquet flooring and the frame of sliding glass doors.

INSTALLATION POINTERS: PARQUET

1 Plan the layout of your parquet floor carefully. Precision measurements at this stage are imperative. To find the starting points for laying the blocks, square off the room with chalk lines snapped from opposite corners or the midpoints of opposite walls.

2 Check the lines with a carpenter's square. When you are satisfied with the accuracy of your measurements, tack down 1x2s to act as guide boards. These, too, must be at right angles to each other, as shown.

3 Loose-lay the tiles to get a sense of pattern and learn about difficulties you may face at the borders. Alternate the direction of wood grain strips as you work along each row to create the pattern characteristic of parquet floors.

4 Measure the border blocks as explained for resilient tile, on page 111. Allow a ½-inch gap at the wall edge for expansion. Parquet flooring can be cut either with or across the grain, using a utility or linoleum knife.

WOOD STRIPS AND PLANKS

INSTALLATION POINTERS: STRIP FLOORING

1 Lay the first wood strip so the groove is aligned with the baseline. Use scrap wood to protect the expansion gap. Blind-nail through the tongue every 12 to 15 inches along the board. The next board will hide the nails.

2 Carefully measure the distance needed to finish each course before cutting the last piece. Take care not to cut off the tongue or groove needed at one end. Also remember to subtract ½ inch from the measurement to allow an expansion gap.

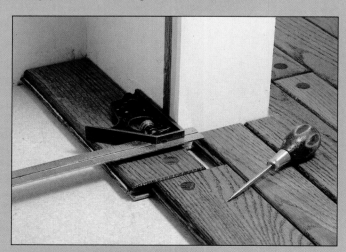

4 When you must fit a board around an irregular shape, such as a doorway, measure with a combination square, as shown. Scribe the cutout for a perfect fit. For a curve, scribe with a compass.

5 Use a coping saw, saber saw, or jigsaw to cut along the scribed lines. A C-clamp will help hold the piece steady on a work surface as you make the cut. Protect the face of the strip from the clamp with a small piece of scrap wood.

3 Use a buffer block—a scrap piece of flooring—to tap the boards together into parallel alignments before beginning to nail each successive course. The block protects the tongues from being damaged by a hammer blow. Work the full length of the board before nailing.

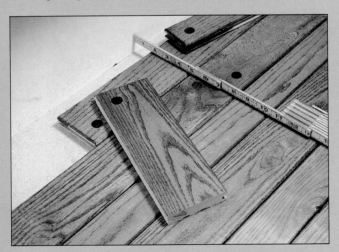

6 To fit the last strip, pull the last few courses of flooring tight with a pry bar, protecting the wall with a piece of scrap wood. Cut the last strip to fit, again allowing ½ inch for expansion. Face-nail the board's surface to secure the last course in place. Install base moldings.

Wood strips or planks are not as easy or quick to install as parquet blocks, but they are among the all-time favorite flooring materials. You can even install them yourself—with time and patience.

Like parquet, wood strips and planks should be stored in your house for at least three days before installation. Break open the bundles the wood comes in and spread the strips around the room they will go in. This will expose all pieces to the humidity conditions in your home.

Underlayment

Like most other types of flooring, wood needs a sound base beneath it. The subfloor does not, however, have to be quite as carefully prepared as for more brittle materials such as hard-surface tiles. If you are putting down strip or plank flooring over existing wood or resilient flooring that's in good condition, you don't need an underlayment.

If the existing floor is in bad condition, however, then you will need underlayment if you want the new floor's good looks to last. If the old floor is made of ceramic or other breakable tile, remove it before putting down underlayment; for most other materials, you can install underlayment on top of the existing floor. The dimensions of the strips and the way they will be installed determine what the best underlayment would be. Check with your supplier. Your local building code may also have something to say on this subject.

Make sure that the floor or subfloor to be covered is thoroughly clean and smooth. Repair any squeaky spots or irregularities, and reset popped nails. Use building paper to smooth out minor irregularities on the existing wood surface.

Finding the baseline

The first step, as with other types of flooring, is to plot a baseline that will serve as a starting point for laying the first boards. Because few rooms are perfectly square, you must make allowances for any discrepancies; the idea is to make baseboards and floorboards *look* parallel.

To find the baseline, measure between opposing walls at 3-foot intervals. If the measurements are within ½ inch of each other, you can make a simple baseline. Measure the full width of one board plus an allowance of ½ inch for expansion. Repeat this procedure at the other end of the room, and snap a chalk line.

If the room is out of square by more than ½ inch, you'll have to draw a balanced baseline to distribute the difference gradually along the length of the room.

Basic procedures

For stability, wood strips and planks are usually run parallel to the longest wall of the room, but they can also go in diagonally or at right angles to the longest dimension. As a rule, however, they should be perpendicular to the floor joists.

If you use a power nailer—available from tool rental companies—you will be able to lay several hundred square feet of flooring a day. Whether you are using this tool or working with a hammer, the nails should be driven into the tongue of each board at a 45-degree angle. The groove of the next board then slides over the tongue of the first and hides the nails.

FINISHING WOOD FLOORS

Once your new wood floor is installed, one all-important task remains: finishing. Much of the beauty and durability you expect from a good wood floor comes from the way it's sanded and sealed.

Keep in mind that the same techniques used to finish a newly installed wood floor can revive and rebeautify an existing wood floor. If you are refinishing an existing floor rather than finishing a new one, you also have to remove the old finish and any mars or scratches acquired over the years, which means more sanding than you would do with a new floor.

Whatever the age of your wood floor, finishing or refinishing it will be a messy and time-consuming process. Whether you decide to do the job yourself or hire someone else to do it, be prepared to have your household disrupted for several days.

Preparation

Remove all furniture and rugs from the room or rooms to be finished. Also remove window treatments and base moldings. Set any popped nails below the floor surface: If they protrude, they'll shine like new pennies after you sand.

If you plan to paint or wallpaper the room, do so before you finish the floor. That way you won't have to worry about drips and spills spoiling the new finish.

Before you undertake any sanding, seal off the work area from the rest of the house. Dampened sheets hung over doors work well to catch and contain dust. Tape paper or plastic over any heating air returns and pack registers with newspaper to keep dust out of the system. Wear a respirator to protect your lungs.

Equipment

If you decide to do the work yourself, you will need to rent a few pieces of equipment—an upright drum sander for the main floor area and other open spaces, and a disk-type edge sander, also known as a Goge sander, for sanding along the baseboards. For polishing the floor after each coat of sealer or finish, you'll need a polishing machine. The rental agency should also supply you with sandpaper.

Check with local rental places to see whether you should reserve the equipment in advance. In any case, be sure to pick up the equipment early in the day to make sure you have enough time to do all the work you plan to do.

When you pick up the equipment, have the dealer demonstrate how the machines work. They are powerful and capable of damaging wood, and your floor is no place for experiments. Be sure you learn how to put the sandpaper snugly on the drum sander; incorrectly installed paper will tear, and paper is expensive.

Sanding

Begin with the drum sander. Always rock it back as you begin and end each pass, to avoid gouging the floor. Never sand directly across the wood grain. Three cuts with the grain will give most floors a smooth surface, but if the floor is in bad condition, you may need to make four cuts, the first two diagonally and the last two with the wood grain. Use progressively finer sandpaper with

FLOOR FINISH OPTIONS

	COST	DURABILITY	APPLICATION
POLYURETHANE	The most expensive wood-floor finish. Use less-costly high-gloss for base coats; top with high-price satin finish.	Impervious to water, alcohol, grease, and general dirt. Extremely durable and mar-resistant, but scratches easily. Once scratched, the surface is difficult to touch up.	Use a natural-bristle brush with a chiseled point, or a spray gun, which can be rented. Do not apply over shellac.
NATURAL-RESIN VARNISH	Prices range from inexpensive to moderate, depending on the quality of the varnish and whether it is clear or a stain.	Very durable and resistant to scuffs and scratches. More susceptible to water damage than polyurethane finishes are.	Apply with a special varnish brush. Thin with recommended solvent. Make sure no dust is present, and avoid formation of air bubbles.
RESIN-OIL SEALERS	Prices range from moderate to expensive.	Resistant to stains, burns, scratches, water, and alcohol. Oil penetrates into the wood and hardens the grain. Easy to repair.	Two or three coats are usually needed, applied by hand with a clean cotton cloth.

Check the floor carefully for bumps and depressions, and hand-sand them smooth. Then vacuum the room thoroughly and go over the floor with a tack cloth to pick up any remaining dust.

Types of finishes

There are three types of finishes you can use on your floor: polyurethane, varnish, and penetrating sealers. Each has its strengths and weaknesses.

Since the advent of synthetic polyurethane, it has become a favorite. It brushes and sprays on easily, dries quickly, remains clear, needs no rubbing or polishing, and is highly resistant to the common foes of wood floors—water, alcohol, grease, and traffic. Polyurethane does have two drawbacks, however. Although it is very durable, it also scratches easily, and the scratches are nearly impossible to touch up. Also, it is the most expensive type of wood floor finish.

Natural-resin varnishes are less expensive than polyurethane, but they also are less durable. Available in both clear and pigmented form, they require 24 to 36 hours to dry, compared with the 12 hours between coats needed for polyurethane.

Penetrating sealers made of resin oil have some advantages, and are less expensive than polyurethane, although more expensive than natural varnishes. Sealers soak into the wood grain, hardening it and giving it an attractive low-gloss sheen. Oil finishes of this kind resist stains, scratches, burns, water, and alcohol, and they are easily repaired. To touch up a problem spot on an oil finish, just sand lightly and apply a fresh coat of sealer. Penetrating sealers have two

big drawbacks: They are time-consuming to apply and require more maintenance than polyurethane or natural-resin varnish.

The chart *opposite* provides a comparison of the three major wood-floor finishes.

Finishing your floor

Once the dust has cleared, you are ready to apply the finish to your floor. To apply polyurethane, use a natural-bristle brush or a spray gun. If you are using a brush, stir the polyurethane in its container, then pour off about a quart into the can you will be working from. Work quickly, brushing on the finish with the grain. To prevent lap marks, do two boards at a time. If polyurethane is to go over a stain or a wood filler, make sure the surface is thoroughly dry.

You'll need to apply at least two coats; the first acts as a primer and sealer. Keep your work between you and the light source so you can easily see any areas you've missed. Spots where the polyurethane has not penetrated are nearly impossible to touch up later.

To apply natural varnish to your floor, follow the manufacturer's instructions carefully. The general technique is to apply the varnish with a brush, being careful to avoid forming air bubbles. Try not to shake the can, put too much pressure on the brush, or wipe the brush on the rim of the can. If bubbles do form, get rid of them by applying more varnish and brushing them out.

Resin-oil sealers are usually rubbed by hand into the wood with a clean cloth and given 8 to 12 hours to dry between coats. Rub with the grain, working in small sections. Wipe off excess quickly to achieve the precise degree of coloration you want.

each cut. If you are removing paint or sanding very rough floorboards, start with very coarse 20-grit paper. (The numbers get higher as the paper gets finer.) For sanding new, fairly smooth strip or plank flooring, or parquet, start with 60-grit open-coat paper. The second cut should be with 80-grit open-coat paper. It should be followed by a third cut with 120-grit open-coat paper if the flooring is softwood such as pine, fir, hemlock, or spruce; use closed-coat paper for third cuts on hardwoods such as oak, birch, maple, hickory, or ash. (Closed-coat has more grits per square inch than does open-coat.)

Most old oak floors started out ¾ inch thick and can sustain several sandings. Check the thickness of the old floors in your house by removing a baseboard. If the floors seem thin—parquet, for example, is generally thinner

than wood strips—be cautious. You could wear through to the subfloor. If the flooring has worn thin, use a floor-polishing machine and screen abrasive, which will remove less of the wood's surface.

As you work, alternate sanding with the drum and edge sanders, using the medium- and then fine-grit sandpapers. Be sure to use the edge sander only along the edges of the room: The circular cuts it makes look different from the cuts of the drum sander. An edge sander can gouge the wood as quickly as—or even faster than—the drum sander can, so it demands a steady hand. Keep it moving continuously. As you lower the machine to the floor, start it moving from right to left.

Go over the entire floor twice during the final sanding. Then run your hand over the wood to be sure all sanding marks have been obliterated.

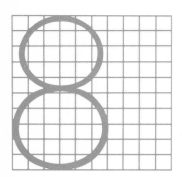

INSTALLING NEW STAIRCASES

Constructing staircases once was the province of master stairbuilders. Today, prefabricated parts and staircase kits have simplified the process somewhat—but installing a balustrade is still difficult. This chapter introduces you to stair-building basics, then takes you through the intricacies of assembling a balustrade. You'll discover whether your own skills are up to this task or whether you'd be better off hiring a skilled professional to do the job. Finally, you'll learn that the techniques for installing a kit-form circular staircase are simpler than you might think.

MAKING AN OPENING

Before constructing any sort of staircase, you need an opening between the levels the stairway will connect. If you're merely replacing an existing staircase, you'll probably tailor the new staircase to fit the opening for the old one, though some modifications may be necessary. If you're adding an entirely new staircase, where the opening should go and how big it should be depend upon your home's floor plan—both upstairs and down—and ceiling height. Chapter 4 covers these basics.

To make the opening, start from below, removing ceiling material, if any, from where the opening will be. Next, determine the opening's corners and drive nails up through the subflooring and flooring; these will serve as guides for marking the opening on the floor above. (Once you know the locations of the joists, you may decide to shift the opening several inches to minimize new joist work.)

Now, making pocket cuts with a circular saw, cut away

flooring and subflooring within the dimensions you've marked. You'll then encounter two or more joists you must cut away and "tie off" with *headers* that run perpendicular to joists; to further strengthen the opening, add *trimmers* parallel to the joists.

Before you make any cuts in the framing of your floor, shore it up underneath with sturdy bracing that runs perpendicular to the joists. Now cut the joists, allowing an additional 3 inches in each direction of the opening for the headers and trimmers you will install.

How you frame an opening depends on whether it's parallel or perpendicular to the joists. The drawings *below* show how to handle an opening perpendicular to joists. For one that's parallel, you'll need to tie off fewer joists with a shorter header.

If you are installing straight-run stairs, don't finish the floor and ceiling around the opening until you have installed the staircase; for circular stairs, the opening can be finished at this time.

PERPENDICULAR OPENING

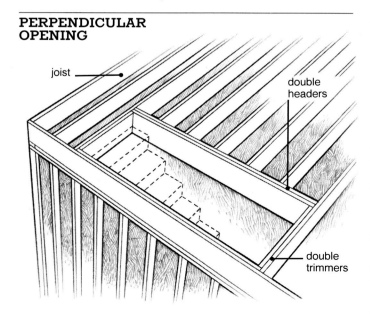

joist

double headers

double trimmers

INSTALLING A STRAIGHT-RUN STAIRCASE

The simplest straight-run stairway is the service type that leads from a home's main floor to the basement, or from a deck to the ground. Built to be purely functional, it usually consists of cleated or dadoed stringers, open treads, and a plain handrail. Basic carpentry manuals can tell you how to construct this type of staircase.

With the components shown on these pages, you or a skilled carpenter can build more elaborate stairways for the main living areas of your house. Whether you choose to do the job yourself or decide to hire a pro depends mainly on whether you need a decorative balustrade, which can be difficult to install, or require only a simple railing.

Many of the parts for a main staircase could be measured and cut from stock dimension lumber, and for years stair makers followed this practice. Now, however, you can purchase ready-made components through lumber and millwork dealers. Though more expensive than stairs built from scratch, prefabricated stairs save lots of trying hours—and possibly wasted materials.

Before ordering straight-run stair components, you'll have to work out specific dimensions. You'll need to measure precisely and determine the total rise and run, the number and depth of treads needed, the stairway width, and the headroom required. (Refer to pages 82 and 83 to learn how to calculate these figures.)

Parts of the whole
Once you're satisfied with both your measurements and your math, you are ready to order components.

Long, notched pieces of lumber called *stringers* or *carriages* form the framework that runs from one level of the house to the other. The stringers pictured here are made of 2-inch-thick pine. *Risers* that are 1 inch thick fasten vertically to the stringers to close in the front of each step. A hardwood *tread,* $1\frac{1}{16}$ to $1\frac{1}{8}$ inches thick, tops off each step. The leading edge of each tread is called the *nosing.* It overhangs the riser providing space for toes.

The handrail assembly, known as the *balustrade,* consists of the *rail,* the individual *balusters* (which attach to the stringers and support the rail), and the *newel* (which anchors the entire balustrade at the bottom of the staircase). The rail begins with an *up-easing,* a piece that runs parallel with the first horizontal step, then curves upward to set the slope the rail will follow.

(continued)

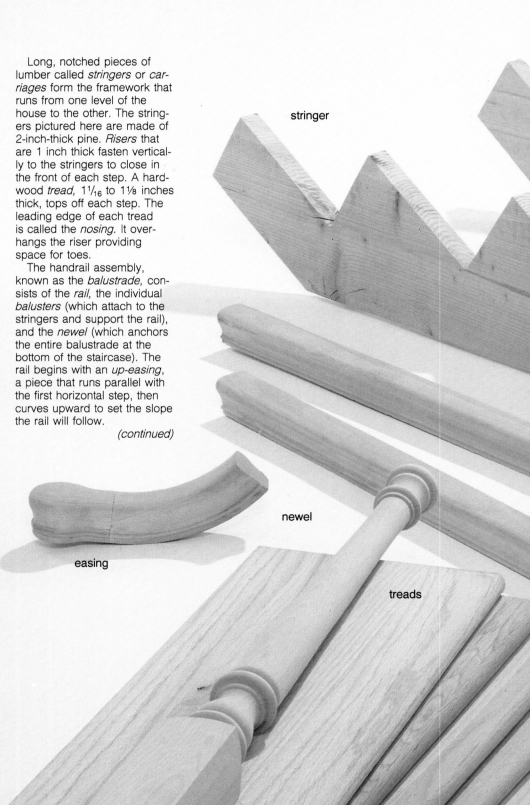

stringer

newel

treads

easing

balusters

risers

handrail

INSTALLING A STRAIGHT-RUN STAIRCASE

(continued)

How did you do in high school geometry? Putting together the components for a straight-run staircase and its balustrade calls for the skills of a proficient finish carpenter—plus an ability to accurately figure angles.

Most of the geometry comes into play when you begin to fit the *easing* that makes the transition from the newel post to the balustrade's handrail; you need to adapt the same techniques shown in photos 5 and 6 *opposite* to make the joint where the top of the railing meets a post or other vertical element at the head of the staircase.

Most stairways in main living areas are at least partially enclosed, with walls on one or both sides and finish material on the underside. Take time to construct such a staircase carefully; once its elements are covered over, getting at them for repairs or modifications is difficult.

Start with the stringers and newel post
Begin by securing the tops of the stringers to the rough opening's header (see the drawing on page 122) and their bottoms to the floor. Position each stringer carefully, then drive nails or lag screws through the header into the stringers. For additional support, drive finish nails at an angle through the stringers into the header.

If you're replacing an old stairway and only the face of the header is exposed, support the stringers with a ledger. Cut a 2x4 to the width of the rough opening, then nail or screw it to the header. Notch the end of each stringer to fit over the ledger, then nail into place.

If your staircase will abut a wall, lag-screw the stringer on that side to the wall's studs and nail through its edge into the floor at the bottom.

Because the newel post anchors the entire balustrade *and* supports the outside stringer, it must be as rigid as possible. In some cases, especially where the outside stringer is unsupported, you may have to carry the newel post through the floor and fasten it to a joist. Otherwise, attach the newel to the stringer with lag screws and glue, as shown in photo 1.

Building step by step
Working from the bottom to the top of the staircase, you assemble steps by first installing the risers, then setting the treads in place, as shown in photos 2 and 3.

To further strengthen the joints, you can fasten 2x2-inch wood blocks on the underside of the staircase where the front of each tread meets the top of each riser. Set each block with glue, then drive two screws through the block into the tread and two into the riser.

Setting the balustrade
Unless you have predrilled stairway treads that will accept the dowel ends of balusters, you'll have to use an electric drill with a spade bit to bore holes. To align the railing assembly, use the newel post as a guide. All measurements for setting balusters should be in line with the center of the newel post so the handrail will be straight when fitted. To make sure they're perfectly vertical, plumb each baluster. Glue the dowel ends into the treads' holes.

Handrails may have either a channel or holes on the underside to accept the top ends of the balusters. Make sure that the rail fits snugly to avoid wobbles later.

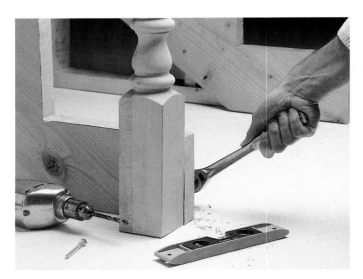

1 Use lag screws and glue to attach the newel post to the bottom of the outside stringer. (Drill pilot holes first.) A secure joint here ensures a safe and rigid balustrade. Some installations may require securing the newel to a floor joist for more stability. Fasten the inside stringer to the wall studs with lag screws along its length. Trim later with moldings.

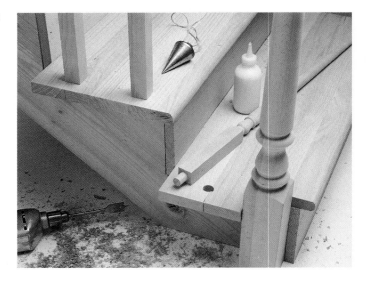

4 Accuracy is a must when setting balusters. Use an electric drill and spade bit to drill holes along a straight line from the newel post to the head of the stairs. Glue doweled ends of balusters into holes in treads using a plumb bob to check vertical alignment. Sometimes treads are notched to accept balusters. In that case, trim molding conceals the joint.

2 Risers tie the inside and outside stringers together and provide nailing surfaces for attaching the treads. To install the risers, predrill nail holes at both ends of each riser, then nail and glue the risers to the stringers. Countersink nail heads and fill with wood putty later. If necessary, plane or file the joints to assure a neat fit against the stringers.

3 Treads fit on top of the stringers and against risers, with rounded nosing facing out. Some stair treads and risers have dado grooves for tighter joints. Drill nail holes through treads into stringers at each side, and through risers into back of treads. Glue and nail. To further reinforce the assembly, fasten wood blocks beneath each riser/tread joint.

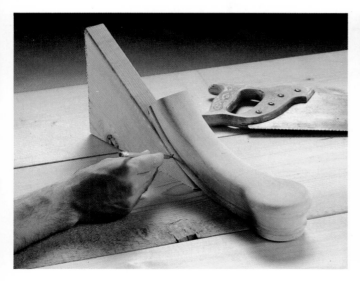

5 To calculate the correct angle for cutting the up-easing, you'll need a pitch block—a triangle of wood with one leg equal in length to the unit rise and the other to its run. Set the easing atop the newel post, level it, and set the pitch block's run side on the level. Slide the pitch block until it just touches the underside of the easing. Mark this tangent point.

6 Flip the pitch block so its rise leg is against the level, as shown, and slide until the hypotenuse of the block intersects the tangent point. Mark this angle; cut it with a miter box. Fasten the rail to the up-easing with glue and a rail bolt—a device that has lag screw threads on the end that goes into the up-easing, and a bolt on the other end.

INSTALLING PREFABRICATED CIRCULAR STAIRS

Compared with the math involved in putting together a straight-run staircase, the computations required to install a circular staircase can be a school dropout's dream. That's because circular stairs are available in kit form, and all the thinking has been done for you. A typical kit has all the parts needed, plus instructions to enable you and a helper to assemble it in a few hours.

Circular stairs are ordered according to their diameter, height, and direction of spiral. Kits range in diameter from 3 to 8 feet, but those less than 4 feet across usually are difficult to negotiate. The rough opening of the upper landing is usually a square cut slightly larger than the stair's diameter. To order the correct height, you need to specify the *total rise*—the distance in inches from the first floor to the surface of the finished floor above. On left-hand spirals you descend counterclockwise; on right-hand ones, clockwise. Your choice depends on the location of the landing and which way you want the bottom step to face.

What's in the package
Much like a giant Erector set, a circular stair kit includes standard pieces, such as those pictured here. The steel *center pole* serves as a common stringer that the *tread supports* hang from. Metal *balusters* attach to *tread supports* and to a continuous *handrail*. A *landing* and *landing rail* complete the staircase's top.

If you like, you can attach optional hardwood treads to the tread supports. A selection of hardware—including lag screws, machine screws, washers, nuts, and toggle bolts—completes the package.

(continued)

handrail

platform

balusters

platform tread

landing rail

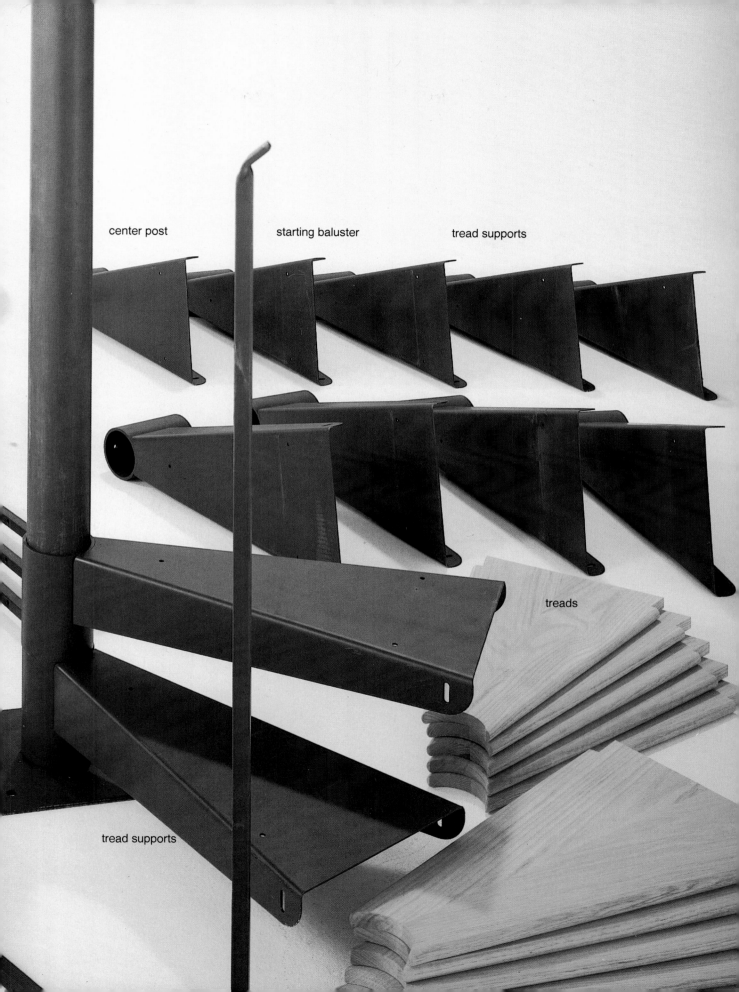

center post

starting baluster

tread supports

treads

tread supports

INSTALLING PREFABRICATED CIRCULAR STAIRS
(continued)

Once you've framed the rough opening (see page 122), assembling a kit-form circular stairway is a breeze. You install the center support pole, drop tread supports onto the pole, bolt a landing in place up top, then position the treads and tie everything together with a pre-cut balustrade. The only tools required to do most of the work are wrenches and an electric drill.

Centering the pole
Correctly centering the support pole is the crucial first step. To find exactly where it should go, decide which corner of the opening you want to connect the landing to, then refer to the chart provided with your kit to determine the proportionate number of inches to mark off for the landing. For example, with a 4-foot-diameter stairway and a rough opening of 50 inches x 50 inches, you would mark a spot 25 inches in both directions from the corner of the proposed landing.

Now lay two pieces of 2x4 across the marks to form an X over the opening. From the center of the X drop a plumb bob to the floor below and mark the spot. Raise the center pole over the mark and pencil in the positions of the baseplate's holes. Drill holes and secure the baseplate to the floor with lag screws. With a level, check to be sure the pole is plumb.

Positioning the treads
Now you're ready to calculate the distance between treads. First measure the exact height from floor to floor. Divide this number (in inches) by the number of tread supports in your kit, plus the landing. The result is the riser height for each tread. (If you'll be covering the tread supports

with wood treads or other materials, for the *first riser height only* subtract the material thickness from the number found above.)

Measuring from the floor up, mark the location of the first riser on the pole. Then continue marking positions of tread supports on up the pole.

Next, stack all the tread supports onto the center pole, alternating them from one side to the other to balance the weight. Loosely install set-screws in the hub (rounded collar) of each tread support.

The landing that comes with a circular stairway kit serves as the topmost tread and also braces the center support pole. Install the landing as shown in photo 1 *at right.* Photos 2, 3, and 4 depict positioning the treads and installing the balustrade. Note that each baluster shapes the spiral by connecting a pair of tread supports.

Finishing touches
All metal parts in a prefabricated circular stair kit come coated with a rust-resisting primer. If you plan to paint the staircase, do it before adding optional tread materials.

Hardwood treads usually come in two designs—*centered* and *flush.* Centered treads are narrower, cut to lengths that cover the tread supports up to a few inches from either end. Flush treads, like the ones shown in photo 5, run from the center pole to the end of the tread supports, covering them completely. To install treads and wood landing platform covers, insert wood screws from the bottom, through the metal supports. If you plan to finish the treads or platform cover, apply varnish or polyurethane before you install them.

1 After the center pole has been erected and the tread supports have been loosely positioned along its length, place the landing platform on the center pole at the last tread riser mark. Align the landing with location marks on the rough opening. Bolt the landing to the header and joist with lag screws. A railing added later will complete the landing.

CUSTOM-BUILT CIRCULAR STAIRS

Kit-form circular stairways come in a variety of styles and configurations, from three-quarter spirals to helixes that make 1¼ turns around the center post. If you don't like the looks of standard kit units, or want something truly special, consider having a circular staircase built to your specifications.

Stair builders can make custom units in wood, metal, or a combination of materials. In some wood designs, the treads' inner-most edges stack one upon another, fanning out like a hand of playing cards and eliminating the center post. Others have serpentine

wood handrails, pencil-thin balusters, and concealed construction tricks so the stairway seems to soar from one level to the next.

Clearly, engineering custom-built circular stairs is no job for an amateur—or even for a professional carpenter with only general construction experience, for that matter. Before you engage an artisan to build a custom stairway, ask to see—and climb—other projects the artisan has completed. Be clear, too, about cost (it will most likely be considerable) and delivery date (good work can take months).

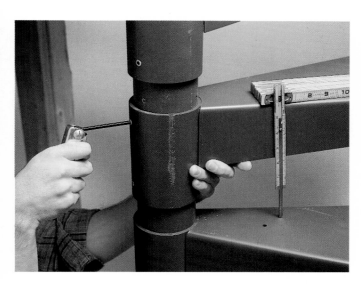

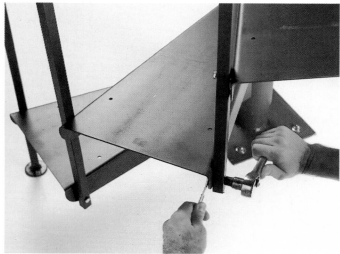

2 With the landing in place, match tread supports with corresponding riser height marks on the pole. Insert screws in hubs to hold supports in position. Use a carpenter's rule to check measurements. At this point, keep screws fairly loose so you can still move the supports around the pole to mate with balusters and assure proper stair alignment in the spiral.

3 Working from the top tread support to the bottom of the stairs, attach metal balusters to flanges in the tread supports with hex-head screws. Each baluster connects the front of one tread support with the back of the next, a method that automatically determines correct tread positions. Plastic plugs and caps cover nuts, bolts, and baluster ends for safety.

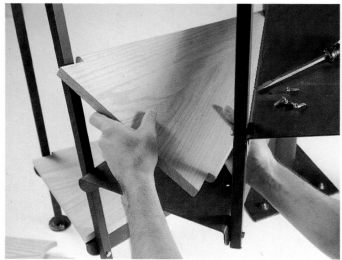

4 Beginning at the base of the staircase, attach the hard plastic handrail to each baluster by drilling a hole and inserting a toggle bolt to anchor it. Check each baluster for plumb before drilling a hole in the handrail. Slip on plastic caps to cover the ends of the handrail at top and bottom. After you install the handrail, bolt the landing rail to the center pole.

5 If you prefer, you can add hardwood treads to metal tread supports. Flush-type treads fit snugly against the pole; centered types require equal spacing from the pole and the step's outer edge. Place treads in position on supports, mark location of screw holes, then predrill holes for wood screws. Apply any finish coat to treads before installing them.

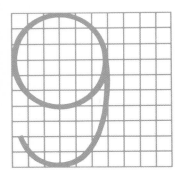

REPAIRING AND REFINISHING FLOORS AND STAIRS

Damaged flooring is always unsightly, sometimes noisy, and often dangerous. Fortunately, many repairs are simple enough to do yourself. In this chapter you'll find solutions to a variety of floor and stair problems.

Understanding how a floor is made and what it's made of is the first step in curing common floor ailments. The illustration *below* shows the basics of floor construction: *joists, bridging, subfloor, building paper, underlayment,* and *finish floor.*

With so many supporting elements to keep it strong, why would a floor develop problems? Moisture in the air is a major culprit in causing wood floors to squeak. It swells the wooden components, and as they dry, they shrink. This makes the boards rub against each other and against the nails that hold them.

If floor joists are exposed to view from the basement, finding the cause of squeaks and moans should be fairly easy. You'll need a person to walk on the floor above you, and a few hand tools (see opposite page). If the subfloor moves over a joist when someone walks directly above it, that's the place to tighten up.

If the subfloor seems sound, see if any of the finish flooring is loose. Have your helper walk over the squeaky part and see if any boards move. If they do, you can try to silence them by forcing such substances as wood glue or powdered graphite between the boards. If that doesn't work, you'll have to nail them. If the ceiling underneath is finished and the joists concealed, you'll have to confront the problem from above, unless you want to remove a portion of the ceiling.

Another cause of trouble is that houses—all houses—settle as they age. Jacking up a sagging house or repairing its foundations is a lengthy job calling for considerable expertise. You'll probably need to call in a professional for help with this problem.

ANATOMY OF A FLOOR

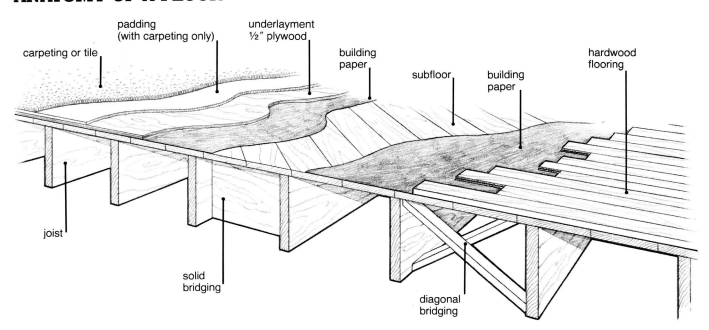

carpeting or tile

padding (with carpeting only)

underlayment ½" plywood

building paper

subfloor

building paper

hardwood flooring

joist

solid bridging

diagonal bridging

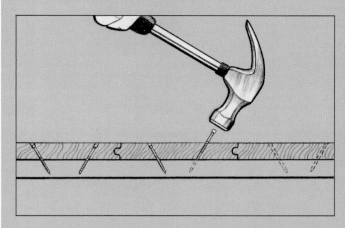

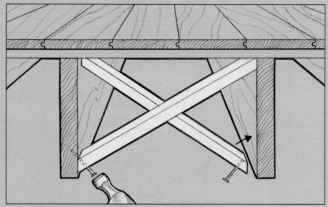

To fasten loose or lifted boards, drive ring-shank flooring nails into the sub-floor. Predrill pilot holes at an angle. Countersink nail heads; fill holes with wood putty, and sand.

Diagonal bridging stiffens joists and keeps them from twisting. Fix loose bridging quickly by pulling the old nails and resetting the bridging with new and larger nails. Replace any split pieces as needed.

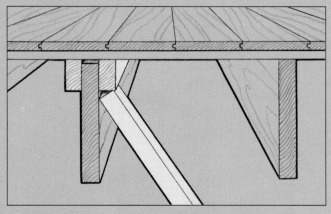

To secure subfloor boards that have lifted, drive tapered shims into the gap above the joist. To do this, dip the tip of the wedge in wood glue, then tap it in until it is snug.

Shore up a series of loose boards by forcing 2x4s against the subfloor. Nail them in place against the joists. Use a prop between the basement floor and the subfloor until you get the nailing done.

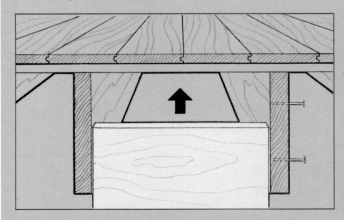

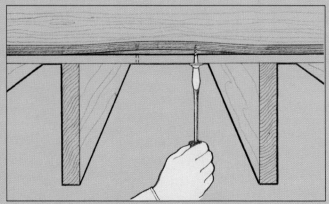

If diagonal bridging keeps working loose, add solid bridging between joists. Every 8 feet of joist span requires a bridge of 2x8s. First, toenail bridging to the subfloor, then end-nail through the joist.

To reset sections of finish floor that have lifted, fit 1-inch roundhead screws from below. Use washers to keep the screws from pulling through later. Drill pilot holes through the subfloor.

PATCHING WOOD FLOORS

Standard wood strip flooring consists of 2½-inch-wide boards with a groove along one end and a tongue along the other. After the boards are fitted snugly against each other, each is blind-nailed into the subfloor at the top of its tongue. If a board becomes warped, split, discolored, or otherwise damaged, you may need to remove it. At other times, removing an entire section of flooring may be the only way to get at faulty wiring or plumbing.

Removing a single board

To remove a single board, drill overlapping holes against the grain and across its narrow dimension. Be careful not to drill too far into the subfloor, or it will be weakened. Use a sharp chisel to split the board down its grain. You can then remove the board without damaging adjacent ones.

Smooth off the rough edge of the hole and cut a new board to fit. Chisel off the lower half of its groove to fit over the tongue of the adjoining board. Then insert the board into place, its tongue and groove coated with glue. Fasten the new board by driving nails through predrilled pilot holes. Be sure to countersink the nails and fill the holes with wood putty.

Removing a section of flooring

If you need to remove more than one board, the job is a little more complicated, but still within the ability of most do-it-yourselfers. The illustrations on these two pages give you a step-by-step view of how to remove a section of strip flooring.

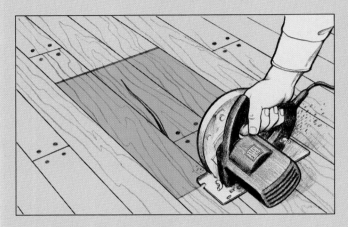

1 With a metal framing square, outline the area you need to remove. Then make a pocket cut along the outline with a circular saw. Use an old blade or one capable of cutting nails, because you're sure to hit some. Since the new flooring will have to butt perfectly with the old, be sure to make the cut straight and smooth.

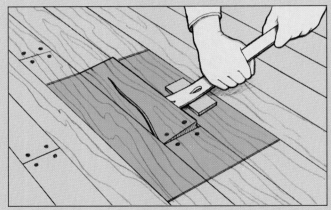

2 Insert a pry bar between two of the damaged boards in the section. Work it back and forth until one of the boards lifts. Because the boards are nailed in place, you'll have to work each one loose. Take care not to damage good flooring next to the section you're working on. Check the edges and corners of the cut for any roughness that would prevent a good match.

3 For an even and neat-fitting patch, you will have to pull out any nails in the opened area, or sink them below the surface. Check the evenness of the underlayment or subfloor, using a flat piece of cardboard if you suspect any unevenness. You can remedy a raised spot from below (see page 133); use countersunk screws from above if the raised spot is over a joist.

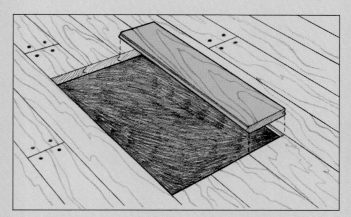

4 If the rest of the floor has building paper under it, cut a section of paper to fit. Glue or staple the paper into place. Measure and cut the new boards for the patch. They should fit tightly. Slip each board into the patch.

Slip the groove of each new board into the tongue of the preceding one, until one board remains to be done.

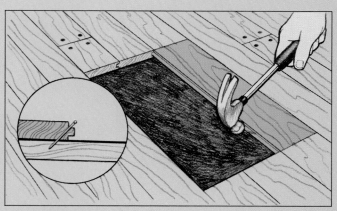

5 Each board will fit into its neighbor like an interlocking puzzle. As you go, blind-nail the boards in place by driving flooring nails through the tongue at a 50-degree angle into the subfloor. The groove of the next

board will fit over and hide the nail heads. If the wood splits easily, drill pilot holes slightly smaller than the nails themselves.

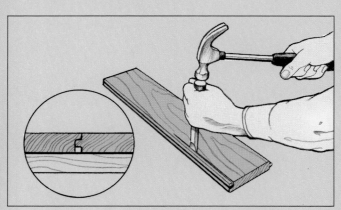

6 Since the last board won't fit—unless half of the groove is removed—turn it over and chisel off the lower section of the groove. It will now lock into place, as shown in the inset. Check the last board for fit. If it is too

tight, try using a hammer and block to tap others into alignment, or sand the board along the edges.

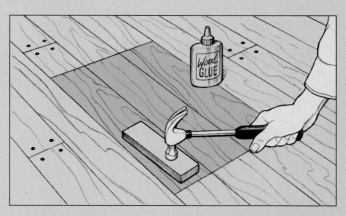

7 It is impossible to blind-nail the last board into place, so you will have to glue it. Spread wood glue on the subfloor and on the tongue and half-groove of the strip. Then tap it into place with a hammer and block to

avoid marring the surface. Wipe off any remaining traces of glue, and weight the piece in place until the glue dries.

REPAIRING RESILIENT FLOORS

RESILIENT TILE

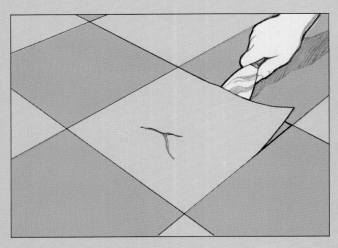

1 To remove vinyl tiles, you need to apply heat to soften the adhesive; an iron, lamp, or portable hair dryer will do the trick. Once the adhesive has softened, use a putty knife to lift out as many tiles as necessary. Other types of resilient tiles—and nonresilient ones—must be chiseled out in pieces.

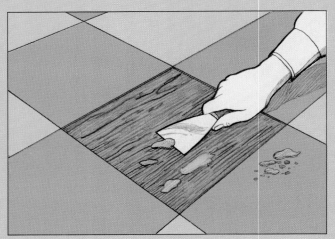

2 For the new tile to lie flat, you must remove as much of the old adhesive as possible from the floor. Again, heat will help in removal. Use sandpaper to take off any adhesive from the edges of adjacent tiles. When you lay the new tile, be sure to use only the adhesive recommended.

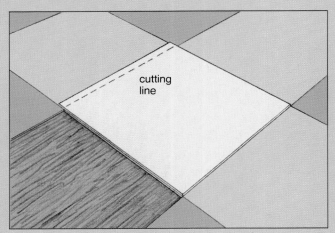

cutting line

3 *Before* applying the adhesive, check the new tile for fit and pattern match. If the tile is a little too large, sand the edges; to take off more than a smidgen, use a sharp utility knife and a metal straightedge to carefully cut the tile. Do not cut on the existing tiles; you may damage the floor.

TILE ADHESIVE

4 Apply the adhesive to the floor as recommended by the manufacturer. Soften the new tile by ironing (use a pressing cloth to protect the surface) or by heating it in an oven. Don't slide the new tile into place. Instead, set the tile on edge against an adjoining tile, then drop it into place. Weight it evenly until the adhesive dries.

RESILIENT SHEET GOODS

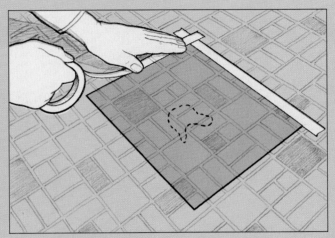

1 Patches on resilient sheet goods can go almost unnoticed if repairs are done carefully. Lay a piece of the same material, larger than the worn or damaged area, over the area that needs patching. Match the pattern, and put tape along the edges of the patching material.

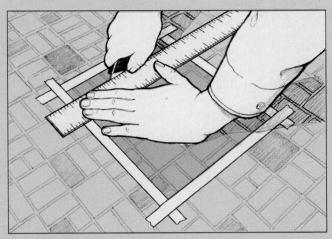

2 With a pencil and straightedge, mark a patch slightly larger than the area the patch will replace. With a straightedge and a sharp utility knife, cut through both thicknesses of material along the lines. Lift off the patch and pry up the original flooring.

3 Remove any adhesive remaining on the underlayment. Fill any holes with patching compound or wood putty. Apply new adhesive with a serrated spreader, or according to directions. Keeping the pattern match in mind, align one edge of the patch and lower it into place. Tap down gently.

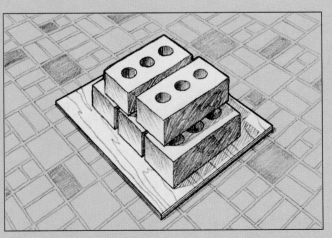

4 Wipe off any excess adhesive that might have oozed up onto the patch surface and surrounding material. For proper adhesion, cover the patch with a piece of plywood weighted with bricks or other heavy objects. Let it dry for at least 24 hours.

REFINISHING WOOD FLOORS

Worn wood floors deserve attention. Besides not looking their best, floorboards whose finish is wearing off are exposed to moisture, stains, and ground-in dirt. To preserve these floors, you must restore the protection the finish provides.

Refinishing usually is difficult. Care and patience, as well as mastery of equipment, are needed every step of the way, or the damage done is likely to rank second only to the original worn floor as an appearance problem.

Sometimes it is too impractical or just impossible to refinish a floor, and replacement becomes a consideration. Common strip flooring, $^{25}/_{32}$ inch thick, remains serviceable after repeated sandings, but it does have its limits. Other wood flooring, only $^3/_8$ inch thick, may become unusable after only a few sandings.

If you do decide to tackle your own floor refinishing, you can rent the needed equipment inexpensively. Because a drum sander, used for sanding the open areas, has a tendency to "run" ahead of the user, its use requires some practice. For more about sanding and finishing, see pages 120 and 121.

Be sure to prepare the floors thoroughly before you start work. Remove or sink protruding nails, and replace any splintered or otherwise damaged wood, as shown on pages 134 and 135.

One special treatment for a floor in need of refinishing is to lighten the wood's natural color. This calls for you to apply two differing grades of wood bleach, sanding lightly between applications to lower the grain. Then comes a coat of neutralizer and a final sanding before the protective finish is put on.

SANDING, REFINISHING WOOD FLOORS

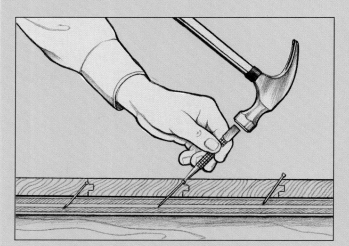

1 Prepare the room for sanding by removing all furnishings and all baseboard shoe moldings. Sink all nails below the floor surface, or pull them. Check for tacks, staples, or other protrusions that might tear sandpaper or damage the sander.

2 Start with coarse paper along the grain. Rock the sander back at the beginning and end of each cut. Otherwise, the drum will bite deep wherever you stop it, creating a depression and possibly damaging the wood irreparably.

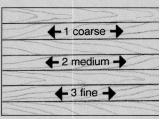

Progressing from coarse to medium to fine sandpaper—with the grain—will smooth most floors.

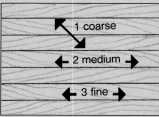

A diagonal pass across the grain takes more off stubborn floors. Do not go directly across grain.

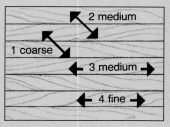

Rough, cupped old floors may need four cuts to smooth them; be sure always to overlap passes.

3 Disc sanders, or floor edgers, can reach where drum sanders cannot. Their circular cut is so different from a drum sander's, however, that you should never operate disc sanders in open areas. To get at tight spots and low areas inaccessible even to a disc sander, use a hand sanding block.

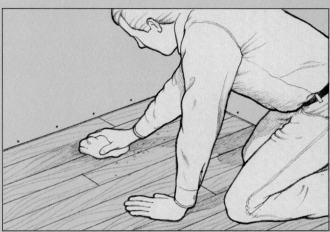

4 Any fine dust that remains on the floor will mar the final finish, so vacuum thoroughly with a brush attachment after sanding. Let the dust settle, then vacuum again. Finally, go over the entire floor with a tack cloth to pick up leftover dust.

5 Paste-type wood filler, applied with the grain, will fill freshly sanded wood pores, concealing holes and crevices that would show when finished. When the filler begins to set, wipe across the grain with burlap or a rough towel. Clean up any excess by wiping the floor parallel to the grain.

6 Apply finish with a brush or roller, or swab it on with a saturated cloth. Use a brush along the edges. Let the finish dry 24 hours, then apply a second coat. After the finish is thoroughly dry, coat with paste wax and buff. If you use polyurethane, check with the manufacturer of the finish before waxing.

REPAIRING SQUEAKY TREADS AND RISERS

Except in movie thrillers, stairs shouldn't squeak. In addition to being an annoying sound, stair squeaks can indicate trouble is on its way. A stair tread that works loose, for example, could cause a serious fall. Do not wait until then to take corrective action.

Most stair noises are the result of rubbing between the tread and the top or bottom of a riser, or between a tread and a stringer. A dry lubricant, such as powdered graphite, applied to the squeaky area will reduce or silence squeaks, but that solution is only temporary. For safety and a permanent repair, use screws, blocks, and wedges. Pinpoint any problem areas by shifting your weight on the treads; then use the pointers detailed here to silence them.

A staircase in its simplest form has two stringers running from one level to another, with steps fixed between them. Most homes, however, have at least two variations on this basic type. *Open-stringer* staircases have stringers cut like sawtooths, with the treads and risers attached to them. *Closed-stringer* construction features straight-edged stringers with grooves cut into their inside faces and steps fitted into the grooves. Some staircases have a closed stringer against a wall and an open stringer on the other side.

The type of staircase you have will determine what direction you make the repairs from. Repairs to staircases with one open stringer can often be done from below, as shown in the illustrations *at right*. When both sides are closed, however, you will have to make repairs from above, as shown in the illustrations *opposite*.

OPEN-STRINGER STAIRS

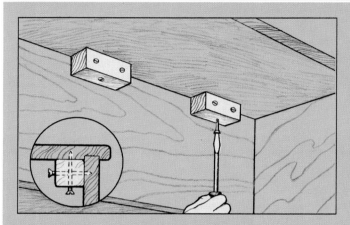

To silence a squeak coming from the bottom of a tread and the top of a riser, install a pair of hardwood blocks where the two parts join. Cut a pair of 2x2-inch blocks, drill a pair of pilot holes in each direction, coat with glue where surfaces will meet, and then secure with wood screws. Fasten the screws in one direction first to draw the joint together.

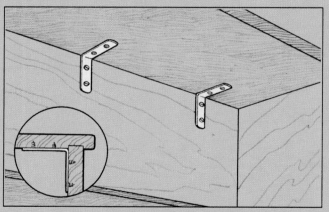

To tighten a tread that seems to be working loose, attach heavy-duty metal angles or shelf brackets at regular intervals along both the tread and the riser below it. An alternative tightening method, not shown, is to use a full-width cleat of hardwood, glued and screwed in place.

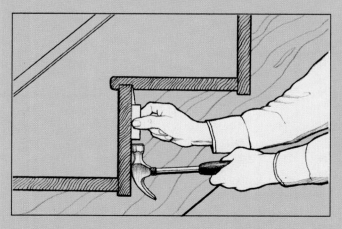

If the existing wedges used to tighten joints come loose, reglue them and tap them into position with a driving block. If the old wedges are in poor condition, as well as loose, make new ones from hardwood. Use no more force than necessary to seat the wedges, old or new, or the tread may lift out of the mortise joint.

CLOSED-STRINGER STAIRS

For a quick fix, apply a dry lubricant such as powdered graphite into the joints at the back of the squeaky tread and the top of its riser. This is only a temporary solution, so be sure to make real repairs in the near future.

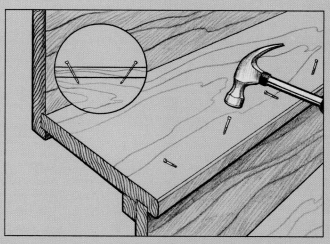

Nailing can silence squeaky tread/riser joints. Drill pilot holes at opposing angles through the tread into the riser. Drive ring-shank nails into holes along the tread. Sink nailheads and fill with wood putty.

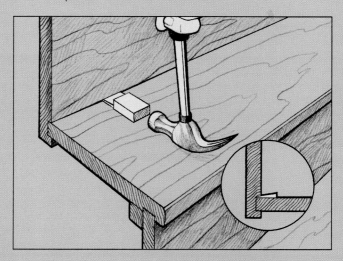

To treat squeaks that originate from the rear of a tread and from the top or bottom of a riser, tap in thin, glue-coated wedges. Cut off the exposed ends with a sharp knife so they are flush.

To tighten loose joints on an uncarpeted staircase, use molding. Nail a section of quarter-round molding into the riser and the stair tread. This will both tighten them and conceal any exposed wedges.

REPAIRING OTHER STAIR ELEMENTS

ANATOMY OF A STAIRCASE

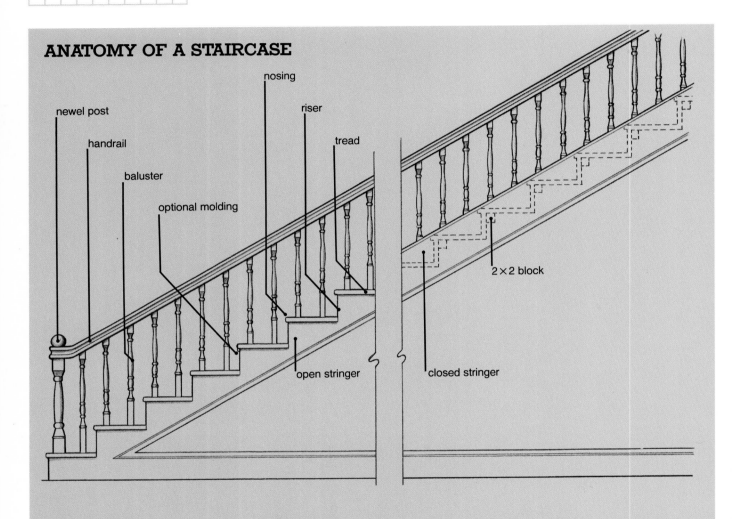

newel post

handrail

baluster

optional molding

nosing

riser

tread

open stringer

closed stringer

2 × 2 block

Add some sophisticated joinery and finely tuned components to the basic open- and closed-stringer staircases described on page 140, and the result is something like the attractive staircase detailed *above.*

Each element that's added, of course, is also an element that can go awry. Additionally, the assorted elements of any staircase—balusters, handrails, stringers, risers, treads, and so forth—can suffer from a variety of ills. Balusters and handrails, for example, can loosen for a number of reasons. The two most common are the gradual settling of the house, which causes stairs to sag and separate from balusters, and undue stress on the rail from shaking or rocking.

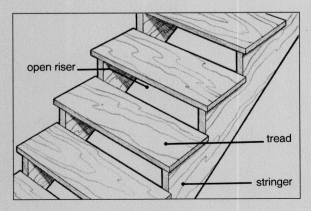

open riser

tread

stringer

Because staircases often are prominent features of a home, dominating the entrance hall or other public rooms, any small aesthetic flaw, such as a missing baluster, becomes very noticeable. Even more important, however, is the safety factor. When a safety device such as a railing is loose or a tread does not provide secure footing, the safety of the entire staircase may be compromised. A wobbly handrail does more than look a bit sloppy—it can lead to a dangerous fall. For that reason, it is important to make sure all the stairs in your home, both the ones that make an immediate impression and the ones that are concealed behind closed doors, are structurally sound.

Typical problems involve either the rails loosening from the balusters, the balusters parting from the treads, or the rail pulling away from the newel post. The techniques shown on this page are adaptable to all these problems, and are within the abilities of many do-it-yourselfers. Other types of repairs, however, are either too time consuming or too difficult for most people to do on their own. A loose newel post, for example, is best left to the care of a professional carpenter with experience in repairs of this nature.

Typical problems

Houses settle as they age. As time passes, this settling may cause the wall and its attached stringer to pull away from the riser-tread construction of the steps. If the resulting gap is less than ½ inch across, you can try to correct it yourself by driving wedges between the wall and the stringer, forcing the latter back into place. A larger gap signals a need to reconstruct the whole staircase—certainly not a job for the average home handyperson.

Balusters integrated by mortises into stair treads can also be a problem. Fix any loose joints by retightening with glue or a hammer and drive block, or by inserting hardwood wedges. Broken treads, however, require the removal of the balusters, separation of treads from risers, and remortising of new wood before rebuilding—again, a job best left to professionals.

Completely enclosed stairways present a more confining and therefore more difficult set of repair circumstances than half-closed stairs do. Repairs to fully closed stairs should be delegated to a pro when the solutions presented in this chapter fail to permanently remedy the situation. Stair repairs can be tricky, so choose your carpenter carefully.

REPAIRING BALUSTRADES

Handrails normally are mounted in one of three ways: holes mortised into them to accept balusters; glued and toenailed to balusters; or supported by wall-mounted brackets. Loose brackets are simple to fix. Just refasten them, or, if necessary, reposition them along the wall and the rail.

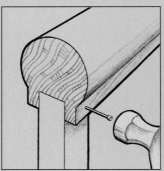

Mortised handrails can be reglued, then stabilized with nails. Shoot a little wood glue into the loose joint and tap the rail lightly into place. Drill pilot holes in the side of the rail so the wood won't split. Drive the nails into the railing and baluster. Don't use the rail until the glue dries.

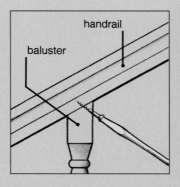

A long wood screw driven at an angle into the handrail or into the tread at the bottom of a baluster will strengthen the assembly. First drill a pilot hole slightly smaller than the screw. For an inconspicuous repair, slightly countersink the screw and fill the hole with matching wood putty. Then sand the putty smooth.

Blocking the underside of the handrail between each baluster will strengthen the entire railing. Cut blocks of hardwood to match the angles. Fit them snugly, then glue and nail them into place. You can also drive small wedges into the gaps at the joints, then trim them off so they are flush.

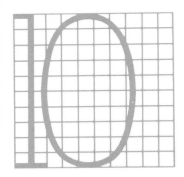

SAFETY AND SERVICE

Attractive as floors and stairs can be, they are basically utilitarian elements of any home, and safety and practicality should never take a back seat to appearance. This chapter tells how to make sure your floors and stairs are safe, how to keep them looking their best, how to provide exits in case of fire, and how to adapt stairs for any disabled members of your family.

HOW SAFE ARE YOUR FLOORS AND STAIRS?

Falling even part of the way down a staircase can be a serious household accident. People can trip over toys abandoned in midflight, or on books stacked at the foot of the stairs waiting to be carried up. This kind of hazard is easy to avoid: Don't let litter accumulate on stairs.

Many falls, however, are caused by design shortcomings in the stairways themselves. To greatly reduce the risk of such falls in your home, make sure all of your stairways meet safety and construction standards. The drawing *opposite* highlights the features you should check.

• *Risers* should be no higher than 7½ inches, for the sake of comfort as well as safety. Open risers present a tripping hazard and should be avoided if children or anyone else prone to stumbling will use the stairs frequently. Keep in mind, too, that every step on a stairway should have the same rise. Uneven heights break your natural rhythm going up or down, causing you to miss a step and fall. Occasionally, however, the bottom riser is slightly lower than the others, because that's where you automatically change your gait.

• *Stair treads* should be at least 9¾ inches deep from front to back. A tread that is too shallow can overbalance a person descending, because an adult's toes will hang too far over the front of the tread.

• *Slope,* or the rise-to-run ratio, of straight-run and other conventional stairs should be no more than 30 to 35 degrees. Anything steeper than 35 degrees makes it hard to keep your balance, particularly going downstairs.

• *Stairway length* is a key safety element. The number of risers in any straight run should not exceed 16. If the distance to be traversed requires more steps than that, try to plan for a good-sized landing in the middle.

• *Handrails* are an essential safeguard. They should run continuously not only between floors but on any flight of stairs having more than three risers. The height of a rail should be 30 inches along the stairway and 34 inches on landings. When attached to a wall, handrails should be set out 1¾ inches to make sure all users have enough room to grasp the railing firmly. Also, a railing should be no more than 2⅝ inches thick—thicker railings are difficult to grasp.

With a staircase that has one open side, the railing should be on the open side. With other staircases, the railing should be on the right-hand side as you descend. That's because more falls occur going downstairs than going up, and since most people are right-handed, placing the railing on their right as they go down the stairs gives them the best chance to effectively catch hold of something if they trip.

Railings should be strong enough to withstand the weight of a falling adult. Ends should not protrude or have sharp edges; they should end in a newel post or a downward scroll or loop.

• *Balusters* should be no more than 5 inches apart, close enough so children can't fall through or catch their heads between them. Uprights can be attached to the stairway stringer; for a more solid hold, however, secure them to the treads. *(continued)*

ANATOMY OF A SAFE STAIRWAY

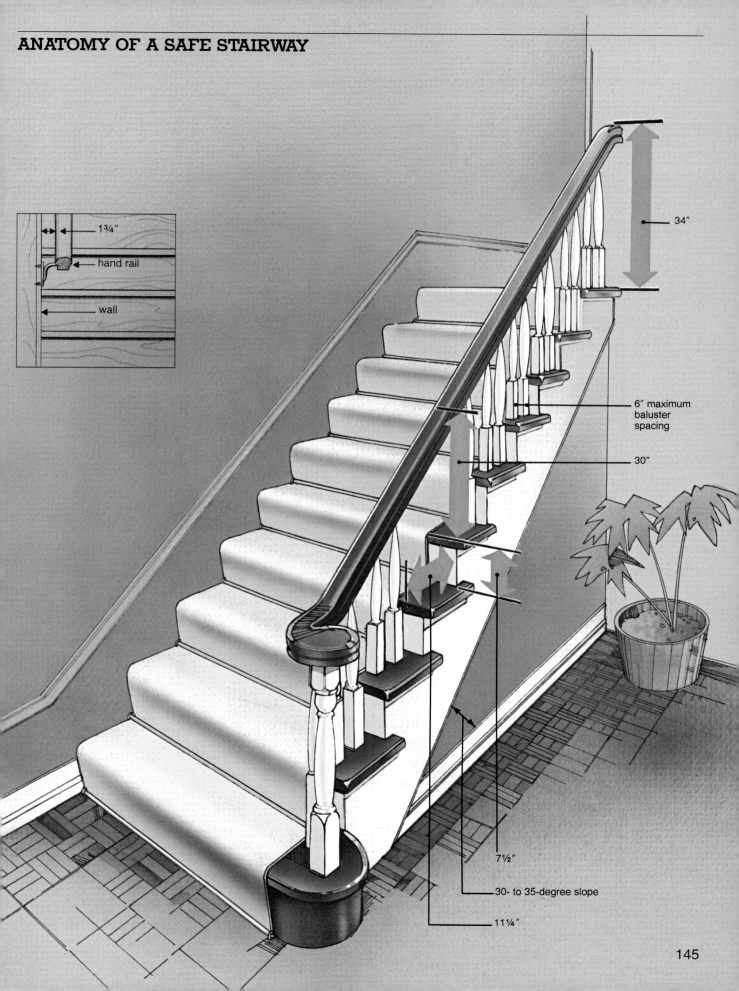

1¾"

hand rail

wall

34"

6" maximum
baluster
spacing

30"

7½"

30- to 35-degree slope

11¼"

HOW SAFE ARE YOUR FLOORS AND STAIRS?

(continued)

The safety features mentioned on page 144 are good places to start when checking the safety of your stairs. For really safe footing, however, consider these items, too:

• *Tread surface* is a vital concern. A slippery tread is a dangerous one, and some surfaces, such as highly polished wood, may be too hazardous for a household that's home to children or the elderly. Do not wax treads. For maximum safety, treat them with a nonslip varnish or with paint that has abrasive additives. You can minimize the hazard of slippery treads by choosing stair coverings carefully.

• *Carpeting* is one of the safest stair coverings, especially if the carpet has a low pile of tightly packed loops. Deep shags can be dangerous, because toes or high heels can catch in the loops.

What's the best way to run the carpet's pile? The answer has to do with a subtle tradeoff between durability and safety. Footsteps, whether they're ascending or descending, exert pressure. If the carpet's pile runs down the steps, the carpet will yield to foot pressure, not resist it, and thus wear longer. On the other hand, if someone in your home is unsteady of foot—perhaps an elderly person—it may be better to run the pile upward, because that little bit of extra resistance will make the surface slightly less slippery.

Some patterned carpeting can be an optical hazard. A flowing design, for example, may run together so one step visually blends into the next. A stripe that runs across the step could fool the eye into thinking the stripe is a step's edge or vice versa.

• *Securely anchored rubber safety treads* are an option worth considering where appearance is less important than safety—on attic or basement stairs, for example. Watch out for smooth rubber, however. When it gets wet it can be as slick as ice. A safer choice is rubber with ribs or other texturing.

• *Safety gates.* If you have small children, make sure to put a barrier or safety gate at the top of all stairways not blocked by secure doors. Many parents also install a second gate at the bottom, so their little ones can't get at the stairs from either direction. Stairs are not safe places for toddlers to play, and it's important to control their access to them.

• *Stairway doors.* In all households, avoid doors that open directly onto the top of a stairway. A door should open onto a landing that is large enough to allow a person room to stand on it when the door is fully open. Otherwise, rehang the door so it swings *away* from the stairway.

• *Broken or missing stair parts* invite trouble. To learn how to tighten up and replace balusters, treads, railings, and other key parts, turn to pages 142 and 143.

On the level

Stairway falls are potentially the most serious, but falls on level flooring also can be painful and hazardous.

• Carpeting that is frayed, worn, or poorly attached makes tripping inevitable. Cushion-backed carpeting held down at the edges with double-faced tape can become wrinkled enough to be a tripping hazard. To prevent this, use a double strip of the tape in front of doorways. Also, if the area has a lot of traffic, lay tape not only around the perimeter but also diagonally, in strips 1 foot apart, all the way across the room.

• Always apply nonslip backing to small area rugs, or secure them firmly to the floor. Use a foam cushion or flat rubberized pad to anchor a large area rug. The padding should be 3 inches shorter and narrower than the rug, or 3 inches less in diameter in the case of round rugs. If you're putting an area rug on top of carpet, use a scrim (woven mesh fabric) underlay beneath the rug. Check rugs to see that the edges don't curl up.

• Loose board and tile flooring also can trip a person. To learn about repairing these, see pages 132–137.

• Floors that have a change in grade from one area to the next can be a tripping hazard if the difference in level is slight. Ideally, the difference between levels should be about the height of a standard riser—6 inches or more. If you have a one- or two-step change in elevation, paint white stripes or use reflecting tape along the top edges of the steps to warn of the change. The metal strips used to bind carpet or resilient flooring edges also can serve as a visual cue.

On the opposite page is a room-by-room survey of a typical home and the special floor and stair safety considerations that apply to each area. Use these checkpoints as a guide to determine how safe your home is underfoot.

EXTERIOR STAIR SAFETY

Because exterior stairways are exposed to weather, you must take care so they don't get dangerously slippery when wet. Here's how to improve traction.

• Remove snow as soon as possible, before it becomes hard and compacted by foot traffic. Sweeping with an ordinary household broom is an effective way to clear away powdery snow; unlike shoveling, sweeping leaves behind no thin, treacherous residue.

• Use textured surfaces wherever possible. Rough-surface brick or stone is more slip resistant than smooth flagstone or marble, for example. Broom-finished or exposed-aggregate concrete also offers extra safety.

• Where frequent icing is a problem, consider heating the treads. Subsurface electrical heating elements and pipes that circulate hot water beneath the surface reduce ice hazards on masonry stairs.

• If your stairs do get slippery because of water, ice, or snow, use sand or other gritty substances to provide traction. (Avoid salt—it will eat away most building materials.) Also, make sure that the railings are strong and easily grasped.

1. Bedrooms

Anchor throw rugs firmly with rubber pads, liquid nonslip coating, or double-faced tape. Arrange furniture to provide clear traffic lanes and to minimize the possibility of tripping over or bumping into items in the dark. Provide a clear and well-lighted path from the bed to the door.

2. Dining room

If an area rug is under the dining table, make sure it is large enough and heavy enough so it won't wrinkle when someone pushes back a dining chair. If the flooring materials in the kitchen and dining room differ, cover the join with a metal or wood strip to prevent loose flooring edges that may cause someone to trip.

3. Kitchen

Keep your kitchen floor clean and dry. Spilled liquids, grease, and granular particles such as sugar and salt make a floor slippery. To minimize the risk of slips, buff resilient flooring often instead of waxing it. Repair broken or loose tiles that protrude above the rest of the floor surface, as explained on pages 136 and 137.

4. Garage

Clean up slippery grease and oil drips right away. Patch holes or cracks and smooth out uneven projections. Make a new garage floor skid-proof by texturing the wet concrete with a stiff-bristled outdoor broom. Use a wire-bristle broom for deeper texture. Coat an existing floor with abrasive paint for slip protection.

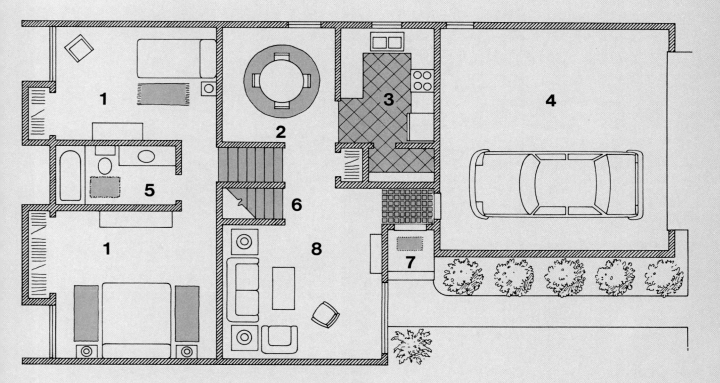

5. Bathroom

Be sure all bathroom rugs are skid-proof. Wipe up water immediately to keep floors from getting slippery. Do not wax any bathroom flooring, whether hard-surface or resilient.

6. Stairs

Keep steps and balustrades in good repair. Don't wax treads. If treads are carpeted, be sure the carpet is tightly attached, and check often to see that tacks have not worked loose. Never use rugs or mats at the top of any stairs, and make sure rugs at the bottom are firmly anchored and not placed loose on a polished surface.

7. Entry

The water-resistant flooring often used in entryways— marble, ceramic or quarry tile, slate, or terrazzo—gets very slippery when wet, so it's important for safety as well as aesthetic reasons to wipe up tracked-in rain or snow right away. Doormats help reduce accidents, provided their edges don't curl up.

8. Living room

Keep traffic paths uncluttered and flooring stable underfoot. Carpets, if adequately padded and properly installed, offer the greatest degree of slip resistance. Replace loose or frayed carpeting and repair cracks, dents, or other defects in wood floors. Use a light coat of nonslip wax on bare wood floors that get lots of traffic.

STAIR LIGHTING

Poor lighting is the culprit in thousands of home accidents each year. Usually the immediate cause is inadequate light, but badly placed fixtures that cast harsh shadows or that create a blinding glare can be almost as dangerous as no light at all.

If you think your stairway lighting is less than ideal, pin down where the problem areas are. Begin by assessing where to place light fixtures to best illuminate each stairway.

Ideally, the first and last steps of each stair run should have bright lighting, with at least moderate illumination for the steps in between. You may need additional lighting at a landing if the lights at the head and foot of the stairs don't reach the center of the run.

Circular or other substantially curved stairways present a special lighting challenge. In the box *at right,* the *leftmost* drawing shows one way to deal with stairs of this type. First, mount a light fixture for overall illumination on a wall adjacent to the stairway. Then install another light at the head of the stairs. Depending on both the layout of the stair area and the appearance of the setting, select a ceiling-mounted downlight or a wall-mounted overall illuminator.

Switchback stairs or L-shape stairs broken by a landing call for another approach to lighting. The *center* drawing shows three fixtures—two ceiling-mounted and one wall-mounted—installed to provide the best possible light on a typical stairway with a landing at the halfway point.

Some stairs are open to natural light from windows or to artificial light in adjacent areas. Totally enclosed stairs, however, are likely to need

their own source of illumination at all times. In a setting of this kind, wall-mounted lights along the stair run, like those in the example depicted *at the upper right* corner of the box, are a sensible choice.

Switching points
The location of light switches is just as important to safety and convenience as the placement of the fixtures themselves. Nearly all building codes require that stairway lighting be controlled by a pair of three-way switches—one at the top and another at the bottom of the staircase. As a general rule, it's best to put switches on a wall immediately adjacent to each entrance to and exit from the stairs. In a split-entry situation, which might have three access points to a stairway, install three *four*-way switches.

At the top of stairs, install a switch so you don't have to lean over the stairway to reach the switch. Otherwise, someone could lose his balance or misjudge the location of the first step.

Extra lighting
If children, elderly people, or persons with poor vision will use the stairs, additional lighting may be in order. For example, consider mounting a series of low-voltage directional lights along the stair runs at each tread. As the illustration *at lower far right* shows, these lights keep the stair tread well illuminated with bright, nonglaring light. Tread lights of this kind are available at most lighting supply firms.

LIGHTING STAIRS FOR SAFETY

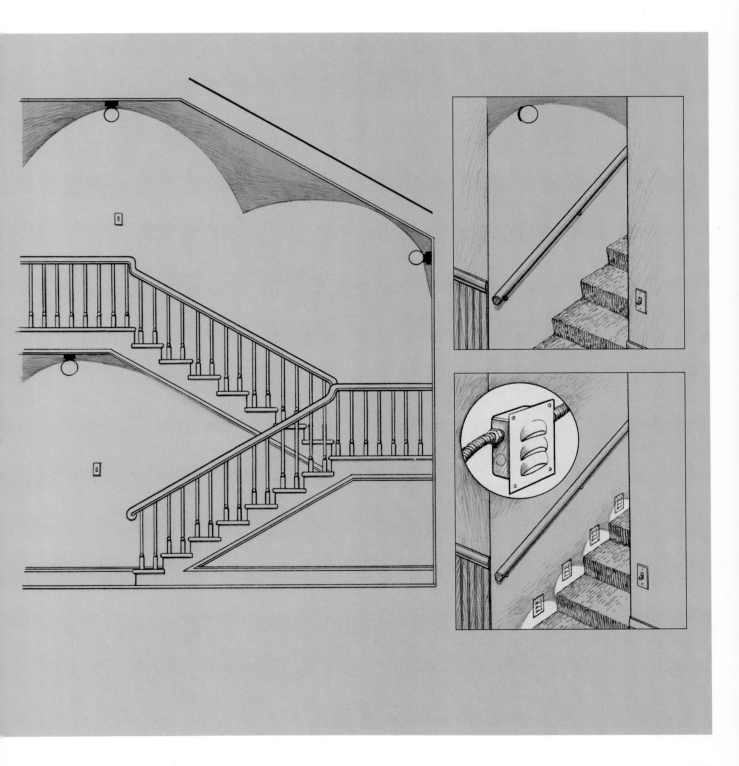

MAINTAINING FLOORS AND FLOOR COVERINGS

CARPETS AND AREA RUGS

Vacuum once a week. Clip, don't pull, loose tufts protruding above the pile level. To raise dents or crushed pile, hold a steam iron above the area and brush the pile.

Blot up liquids and remove solid spills quickly. Sponge any remaining stain with the appropriate solution (see list below), rinse, and blot dry. Always spot-test any solution in an inconspicuous place.
* *Water-soluble stains* (such as alcohol, urine, fruit juices, sugars, starches). If sponging with warm water fails, try commercial carpet shampoo or a quart of warm water mixed with a tablespoon each of mild soapless detergent and white vinegar.
* *Oily stains* (such as grease, cooking oil, butter, face cream). Sponge with a solvent, such as dry-cleaning fluid.
* *Combination stains* (peanut butter, crayon, blood, vomit, shoe polish, tea, milk, coffee). Clean with detergent solution, followed by a solvent.
* *Paint.* Apply turpentine to oil-based paint stains; use detergent on latex stains.
* *Candle wax.* Cover with layers of paper towels and press with a warm iron. Repeat if necessary.
* *Ink.* Permanent-ink stains usually are just that—permanent. Other ink, however, should respond to the detergent-plus-solvent treatment.

Shampoo carpets once or twice a year. A water-extraction—or steam—machine does the best job of cleaning heavy soil and removing residue. The machine forces a chemical solution mixed with hot water into carpet fibers and extracts the dirty water with a high-powered vacuum.

A wet-shampoo machine uses a rotary brush to scrub detergent solution into the fibers. After the solution dries, you vacuum up the residue. This method works if the carpet is not too dirty.

You can also spray on liquid or foam shampoos from a can and scrub with a brush.

For lighter carpet-cleaning jobs and for area rugs, try dry shampoo—an absorbent powder saturated with a chemical cleaner. Sprinkle it on, brush it in, and vacuum. You can also use foam cleaner for area rugs, but don't machine-shampoo them.

Handmade Oriental rugs are a special case; have them cleaned by a specialist once every five years.

WOOD FLOORS

All wood floors, even those coated with polyurethane and factory finishes, can sustain damage from water.

Vacuum or dry-mop wood floors often. Wax lightly and buff floors finished with shellac or regular varnish every three months; wax and buff polyurethane finishes every six months. Use a good solvent-base paste or liquid wax, never a self-polishing or water-base wax. Apply thin coatings each time to avoid wax buildup.
* If water has soaked into the wood, causing a dark stain, sand the area with medium-grit sandpaper. To remove white stains, rub with fine steel wool dipped in mineral oil. Try the same thing for urine stains.
* Remove shallow scratches, dark heel marks, or minor burns with fine steel wool and dry-cleaning fluid.
* Rub chewing gum, crayon marks, candle wax, or tar with ice cubes (in a plastic bag) until the residue is brittle enough to scrape off. Use cleaning fluid to loosen any substance still sticking.

After removing stains, rub the spot with wax or, if necessary, apply a matching finish, feathering it out onto the surrounding areas.

RESILIENT FLOORING

Daily sweeping with a soft broom and occasional damp-mopping will remove ordinary dirt.

Don't overdo resilient floor care. No more often than every three to six weeks, wash floors with lukewarm water mixed with a little ammonia, or mild, nonabrasive detergent. Rinse well; sudsy residue will dull the finish.
* *No-wax vinyl floors* will stay shiny for a long time, but eventually high-traffic areas may lose their luster. Sometimes washing and buffing will restore the shine. If not, apply a thin coat of a special dressing (an acrylic product, not a wax) recommended by the flooring manufacturer.
* *Vinyl without a no-wax finish* needs an occasional thin coat of water-base wax. Fill small holes in vinyl with a seam-welding product offered by manufacturers.
* Clean grease off *rubber* and *asphalt tiles* quickly, and wash with a mild detergent. Seal the pores of asbestos tiles with a water-base wax.

For stubborn stains on resilient flooring, rub with a cloth dipped in alcohol or a small amount of diluted chlorine bleach; rinse. To remove a dent, hold a hair dryer over the spot until it levels.

CERAMIC TILE

Glazed ceramic tiles are fused with an almost impervious glasslike coating. Usually you need only wash the floor with an all-purpose household cleaner. Scrub heavily soiled tiles with a concentrated solution or try a commercial tile cleaner.

Unglazed ceramic tiles are often very porous and may require a stain-resistant sealer. After sealing, tiles usually only need to be sponge-mopped with a household cleaner.

Remove heavy soil or stains on unglazed tile with a paste of scouring powder and water. Mop on the paste, let it stand for five minutes, then scrub vigorously.

To remove some beverage, dye, or fruit juice stains, you may need a chlorine bleach solution (three tablespoons of bleach to a quart of water). Keep the area wet with bleach until the stain dissolves. Scrub iodine and grease stains with washing soda and water. Wipe off soap film with vinegar and water.

Grout between tiles stains easily; you may want to protect it with an acrylic grout sealer. To remove stains from unsealed grout, apply bleach, let it stand five hours, then rinse and dry.

OTHER MATERIALS

Marble, slate, brick, and terrazzo floors should have a sealer coating designed for the specific material. Once the surface is sealed, damp-mop with clear water, and wash twice yearly with a mild detergent solution. Even with this protection, some of these materials still need a few special considerations:
- *Marble* scratches easily and absorbs stains unless resealed frequently. When you wash it with detergent, do small sections at a time, rinsing and drying as you go.

Bleach stains with hydrogen peroxide mixed with a few drops of ammonia. For deep stains, apply a poultice made of powdered whiting (a chalklike substance) mixed to a paste with hydrogen peroxide for organic stains, or with benzene for grease stains. Repeat several times if necessary.

Polish all small rough spots with rottenstone or with aluminum oxide (putty powder), which is available from marble companies.
- *Slate* needs only sweeping and periodic damp-mopping. An acrylic sealer will give it a glistening wet look.
- *Glazed brick* has a baked-on shine, but seal *rough-cut brick* with masonry silicone or liquid acrylic.

Proper maintenance is the best prescription for good-looking, long-lasting floors. The common enemy of all flooring is tracked-in grit. Because it is abrasive, grit cuts carpet fibers, make holes in resilient tiles and sheet goods, and scratches wood and ceramic tile. To avoid this, sweep or vacuum all heavy-traffic areas frequently.

Constant pressure from furniture and friction from foot traffic are other threats. Rearrange furniture occasionally, and shift the position of area rugs so all parts get equally worn.

How often you need to do thorough cleaning, such as shampooing carpets or washing resilient and hard-surface floors, depends on use. A good general rule is never to let any flooring get so dirty that soil becomes embedded deeply in fibers or pores. Clean up spills right away, too. Stains grow more stubborn the longer they set.

Different flooring materials have specific strengths and weaknesses that determine the kind and amount of maintenance they require.
- Some of the new synthetic carpet fibers, for example, are chemically formulated to repel dirt; spills and soil cannot seep into the fibers. Often these carpets are treated with additional soil-resistant finishes and with new antimicrobial finishes that retard the growth of mildew and mold.

Regular vacuuming and an occasional sponging with clear water to remove stains can keep these carpets clean for as long as three years. Other carpets will need cleaning or shampooing about once a year.
- Most new vinyl flooring has a no-wax finish that resists household stains. Solvents and strong scouring powders can ruin the finish, however.
- Other resilient flooring—regular vinyl, asphalt, and rubber—will stain and can be damaged by grease, acids, and solvents.

The box *at left* gives detailed advice about caring for a variety of flooring materials.

When to use a pro

Some problems demand professional treatment. Manufacturers of carpeting, for example, advise professional cleaning of any carpet that is heavily soiled, and of all carpeting at least every four or five years.
- A good professional carpet cleaner will have heavy-duty equipment and chemicals unavailable to the amateur. With these, a professional cleaner can extract old foam and dirt-attracting residues that may have been left by previous home cleanings. In addition, a professional has experience and expertise in coping with special stain and grime problems.

Professional cleaning is expensive, so you'll probably want to supplement it with home cleaning. You can rent or buy equipment that will do a satisfactory job between professional cleanings.
- Resilient and hard-surface floors generally do not need professional cleaning. Deep or extensive stains in marble, however, may not respond to home treatment, and will have to be ground away with industrial equipment.
- Clean and buff wood floors with home equipment you rent or buy.

IN CASE OF FIRE

If a fire occurs in your home, you may be unable to simply stroll out the front or back door, and if you're on a level other than the street floor, you may be unable to use the main staircase to make your exit. For these reasons, it's important to have alternative methods of escape, particularly from upper stories. Several kinds of fire-escape systems can provide for safe emergency departures, enabling you and your family to avoid smoke- or fire-filled hallways and the hazards of delayed escape.

• The permanently installed exterior pipe slide pictured *at near right* offers one way to escape from an upper story. Although sliding down a pipe is not quite as easy as descending a built-in exterior ladder, a pipe makes upper-level windows much less accessible to burglars.

You can build an escape slide of 2-inch-diameter pipe bent or jointed at the top so that a 16-inch horizontal section attaches to the house above a designated window exit. The pipe should be anchored in concrete set in the ground.

• Chain ladders, like the one illustrated *at center right,* are widely available and inexpensive, but, like homemade rope ladders, require that all family members be able-bodied and dexterous. Be sure to store

chain ladders at the agreed-upon exit, ready for use at all times.

To put a chain ladder in place, hook it over the window sill and drop it down the side of the house. Make sure that the window opens easily, is large enough to exit through comfortably, and is never blocked by furniture or other

items. When you purchase a chain ladder, make sure it is equipped with rigid standoffs that keep the rungs far enough away from the exterior wall for adequate hand- and footholds.

• A rope ladder, like the one shown *at bottom right,* offers an inexpensive but serviceable means of escape if all members of your family are

fairly agile and are able to use the rope without help.

To make a rope escape ''ladder,'' tie or clip a knotted rope into an eye bolt permanently fastened to the wall. (If tied, the rope must be left at the designated exit.) To provide hand- and footholds, tie knots about every 12 inches along the length of the rope.

FIRE-ESCAPE SYSTEMS

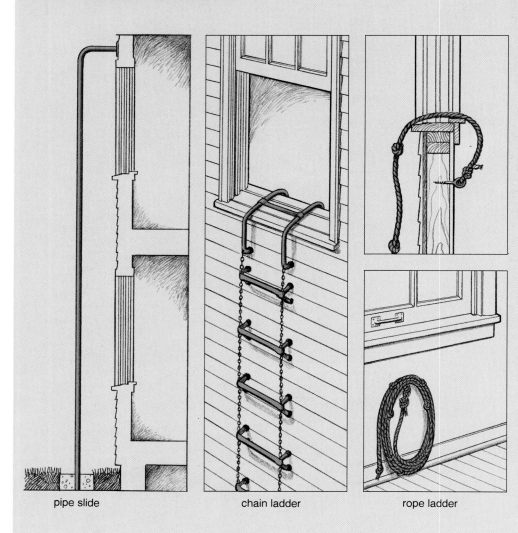

pipe slide   chain ladder   rope ladder

FIRE-ESCAPE ROUTES

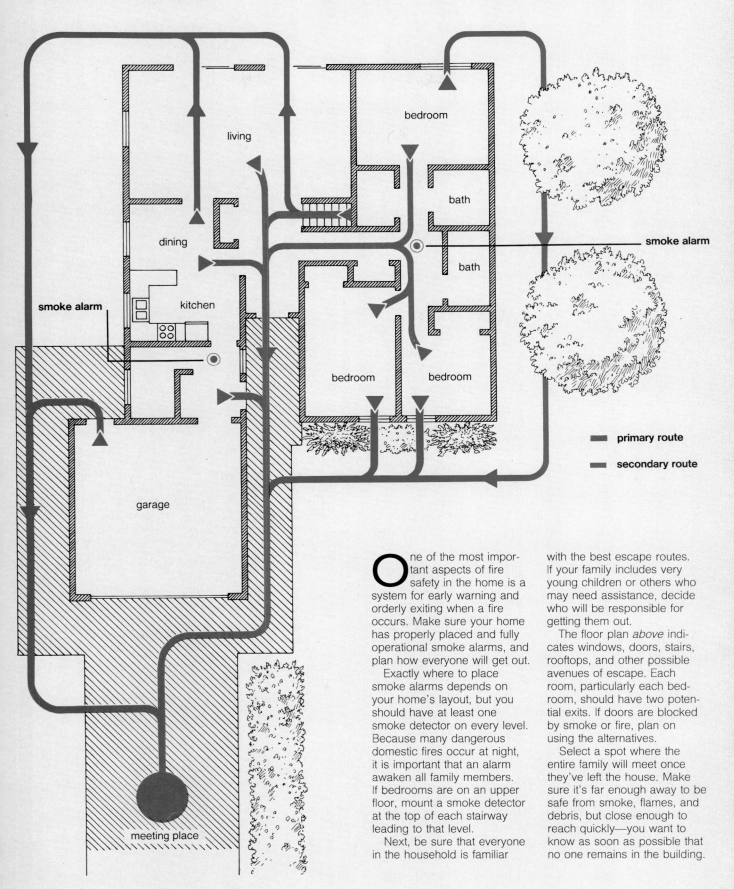

living

bedroom

bath

smoke alarm

bath

dining

kitchen

smoke alarm

bedroom

bedroom

garage

■ primary route

■ secondary route

meeting place

One of the most important aspects of fire safety in the home is a system for early warning and orderly exiting when a fire occurs. Make sure your home has properly placed and fully operational smoke alarms, and plan how everyone will get out.

Exactly where to place smoke alarms depends on your home's layout, but you should have at least one smoke detector on every level. Because many dangerous domestic fires occur at night, it is important that an alarm awaken all family members. If bedrooms are on an upper floor, mount a smoke detector at the top of each stairway leading to that level.

Next, be sure that everyone in the household is familiar with the best escape routes. If your family includes very young children or others who may need assistance, decide who will be responsible for getting them out.

The floor plan *above* indicates windows, doors, stairs, rooftops, and other possible avenues of escape. Each room, particularly each bedroom, should have two potential exits. If doors are blocked by smoke or fire, plan on using the alternatives.

Select a spot where the entire family will meet once they've left the house. Make sure it's far enough away to be safe from smoke, flames, and debris, but close enough to reach quickly—you want to know as soon as possible that no one remains in the building.

STAIRWAY ALTERNATIVES FOR THE DISABLED

Many wheelchair-bound people are capable of impressive athletic achievements, but negotiating stairs is one activity virtually impossible for them to manage. For this reason, access by a wheelchair-bound person to any off-grade building is likely to depend on ramps.

An entrance ramp for access to an exterior door can be built of a variety of materials—wood, concrete, or even earth. Safety and ease of use are the primary criteria, but appearance also can be a factor, especially for a ramp that's visible from the street. Whatever building material you

choose, make sure that the surface the wheelchair will operate on is a nonskid material such as rubber matting or roughened concrete.

As the large drawing *below* shows, a ramp looks very much like a standard pathway in profile. The slope of a wheelchair ramp must be gradual—no more than 1 foot in 12. A total rise of 2 feet, for example, requires a total length of at least 24 feet.

No ramp should be more than 30 feet long without a landing: Landings give wheelchair users a place to rest and to maneuver the chair. Whether your plan is for an

L-shape, switchback, or broken straight-run ramp, all landings must measure at least 5x5 feet.

The base and top of a ramp should have landings, too. Where doors open outward, the top ramp should measure at least 5x6½ feet. This gives room to move the chair back as the door is opened.

Landings must be level enough to prevent the wheelchair from rolling backward when its occupant stops to rest or change direction. Keep in mind, however, that landings should have a slope of ⅛ inch per foot in order to allow for proper drainage.

Handrails on both sides of the ramp allow a wheelchair user to pull the chair up the ramp rather than push the wheels. The most convenient distance for the rails is about 32 inches above the ramp and 1½ inches from the nearest wall. Rails should have a grip width of 1½ inches.

A ramp must be wide enough to accommodate the wheels of the chair, the arms of the user, curbs on either side to keep the wheels from rolling off the ramp, and the handrails. Allow at least 36 inches from side to side between both the curbs and the handrails.

RAMPS

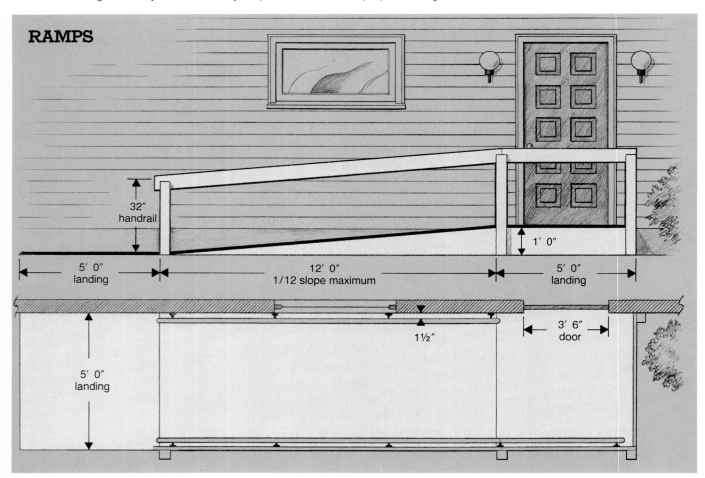

32" handrail

1' 0"

5' 0" landing

12' 0" 1/12 slope maximum

5' 0" landing

1½"

3' 6" door

5' 0" landing

For disabled persons not confined to wheelchairs—those who have restricted movement of a knee, ankle, or hip, for example—specially designed stairs may be the answer. Features, as shown in the drawing *below* should include a nonskid surface and risers no more than 7 inches high, a 1½-inch indentation where treads meet risers, and a handrail 32 inches above the stair surface.

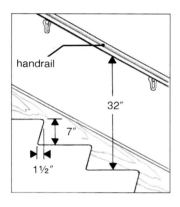

Changes in levels need to be dealt with indoors as well as out. For changes involving just a riser or two, a wooden ramp will provide wheelchair access from one part of the structure to another.

Where it is impossible to install an indoor wheelchair ramp, consider a stair tram, like the one pictured *at right*. Stair trams transport a seated person up or down stairs. Installation of various models, seating one or two people, requires only minor changes to existing stairs.

An extruded aluminum channel attached to the stairs serves as the track that the seating section glides on. A power unit, which operates on 110-volt household current, can be installed at the head or foot of the stairs or in the basement. Call and send controls go at both the head

A STAIR TRAM

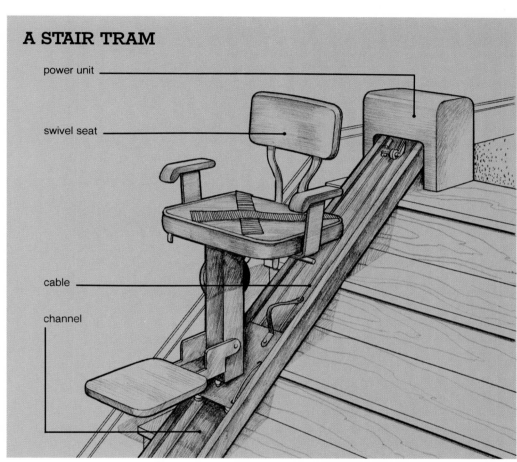

and foot of the stairs. A control button on the tram itself operates the lift.

Seat belts are standard safety features. Some models have swivel seats for easy entrance and exit. Some even have hand cranks so they can operate in case of power failure. Other options include food trays, handles, and special seat widths.

Stair trams can be mounted on either the right or left side of the stairway. Models that fold back toward the wall when not in use (like the one illustrated *at right*) allow free foot access to the stairs.

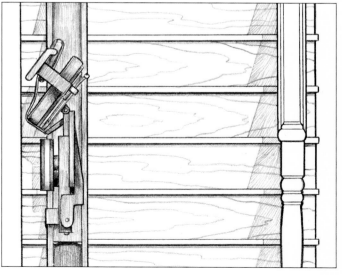

YOUR FLOORS & STAIRS

WHERE TO GO FOR MORE INFORMATION

Better Homes and Gardens® Books
Would you like to learn more about your house? These Better Homes and Gardens® books can help.

Better Homes and Gardens®
NEW DECORATING BOOK
How to translate ideas into workable solutions for every room in your home. Choosing a style, furniture arrangements, windows, walls and ceilings, floors, lighting, and accessories. 433 color photos, 76 how-to illustrations, 432 pages.

Better Homes and Gardens®
DOLLAR-STRETCHING DECORATING
An excellent source for ideas and projects that make your dollar work harder. Shows how to use imagination, ingenuity, and know-how to sidestep high costs while stepping up in style, comfort, and quality. Filled with easy-to-accomplish ideas, practical suggestions, do-it-yourself projects, and how-to drawings. 192 pages.

Better Homes and Gardens®
COMPLETE GUIDE TO HOME REPAIR,
MAINTENANCE, & IMPROVEMENT
Inside your home, outside your home, your home's systems, basics you should know. Anatomy and step-by-step drawings illustrate components, tools, techniques, and finishes. 515 how-to techniques; 75 charts; 2,734 illustrations; 552 pages.

Better Homes and Gardens®
STEP-BY-STEP BUILDING SERIES
A series of do-it-yourself building books that provides step-by-step illustrations and how-to information for starting and finishing many common construction projects and repair jobs around your house. More than 90 projects and 1,200 illustrations in this series of six 96-page books:
STEP-BY-STEP BASIC PLUMBING
STEP-BY-STEP BASIC WIRING
STEP-BY-STEP BASIC CARPENTRY
STEP-BY-STEP HOUSEHOLD REPAIRS
STEP-BY-STEP MASONRY & CONCRETE
STEP-BY-STEP CABINETS & SHELVES

Other Sources of Information
Many manufacturers and associations publish catalogs, style books, or product brochures that are available upon request.

American Olean Tile Company
Public Relations Department
1000 Cannon Avenue
Lansdale, PA 19446

Armstrong World Industries
(resilient flooring)
Consumer Services
P.O. Box 3001
Lancaster, PA 17604

Bruce Hardwood Floors
Marketing Department
16803 Dallas Parkway
P.O. Box 220100
Dallas, TX 75222

Carpet Cushion Council
P.O. Box 465
Southfield, MO 48037

Carpet & Rug Institute
P.O. Box 2048
Dalton, GA 30720

Congoleum Corporation
Resilient Flooring Division
195 Belgrove Drive
Kearny, NJ 07032

Duvinage Corporation
(spiral, circular, and kit stairs)
P.O. Box 828
Hagerstown, MD 21740

Tile Council of America
Box 326
Princeton, NJ 08540

Vermont Marble Company
61 Main Street
Proctor, VT 05765

ACKNOWLEDGMENTS

Architects and Designers
The following is a page-by-page listing of the architects and designers whose work appears in this book.

Pages 6-7
Surber & Barber
Pages 8-9
Suzanne Worsham, Patience Corner, Marilyn Hannigan
Pages 10-11
Kenneth R. Nadler, A.I.A.
Pages 12-13
Irv Weiner
Pages 14-15
Leslie Armstrong
Pages 18-19
Fittings, Inc.
Pages 20-21
Barry Berkus
Pages 22-23
Candler Lloyd Interiors
Page 24
Tony Garrett, Jeff Hicks
Page 25
Richard W. Robb & Assoc.
Pages 26-27
Phyllis Schwartz
Page 28
Michael La Rocca
Page 29
Hanne Brenken,
Ricardo Wiesenberg
Pages 30-31
Robert Braunschweiger
Page 32
Bill Lewis
Page 33
Eugene Fulterman

Pages 34-35
Donna Warner
Page 36
Peter David Di Pietro
Page 37
John Sampieri, A.I.A.
Pages 38-39
Cardone Interiors
Page 40
Betty Roberts
Page 41
Jova/Daniels/Busby
Architects
Kathy Guyton Interiors
Page 42
Alexander Dekker, A.I.A.
Aase Gilbertson Interiors
Page 43
(left) Tricia Jasper, A.S.I.D.
(right) Bow House, Inc.
Page 45
Timothy B. Fox
Page 48
Clem Labine
Page 49
Craig Stewart
Page 52
Ast-Dagdelen

Page 53
Donald Parker, A.I.A.
Page 54
Adek and Doris Apfelbaum
Page 55
Dory David, Dorothy Collins
Interiors
Pages 56-57
Western Wood Products
Association
Page 58
Thomas Scott Dean, A.I.A.
Page 60
Thomas H. Olson
Page 61
Michael Cox, The Wold
Association
Page 63
Nano Turchi, A.I.A. and
Richard Caldwell, A.I.A.
Page 64
Garth Graves
Page 65
Roberts Associates
Page 68
Linda Brock
Page 69
(top left) Bob Kirkland
(top right) Robert Thompson,
Hanson Dunahugh Vaivoda
Thompson Nicholson, A.I.A.
(bottom left) J. Carson
Bowler and John F. Cook,
A.I.A.
(bottom right) Linda Brock
Page 70
Ed and Nancy Uselmann
Page 72
Milton Schwartz

Photographers and Illustrators
We extend our thanks to the following photographers and illustrators whose creative talents and technical skills contributed much to this book.

Mike Blaser
Ross Chapple
George de Gennaro
Jim Hedrich, Hedrich-Blessing
Bill Helms
William N. Hopkins,
Hopkins Associates
Fred Lyon
E. Alan McGee
Carson Ode
Maris/Semel
Jessie Walker

Associations and Companies
Our appreciation goes to the following associations and companies for providing information and materials for this book.

Armstrong Cork Co.
Des Moines Marble and
Mantel Company
Duvinage Corporation
Flexco, a division of Textile
Rubber Company, Inc.
Rowat Cut Stone Company
Vermont Marble

INDEX

Page numbers in *italics* refer to photographs or illustrated text.

Have BETTER HOMES AND
GARDENS® magazine
delivered to your door.
For information, write to:
MR. ROBERT AUSTIN
P.O. BOX 4536
DES MOINES, IA 50336